Combating the Achievement Gap

Combating the Achievement Gap

Ending Failure as a Default in Schools

Teresa D. Hill

ROWMAN & LITTLEFIELD
Lanham • Boulder • New York • London

Published by Rowman & Littlefield
A wholly owned subsidiary of The Rowman & Littlefield Publishing Group, Inc.
4501 Forbes Boulevard, Suite 200, Lanham, Maryland 20706
www.rowman.com

Unit A, Whitacre Mews, 26-34 Stannary Street, London SE11 4AB

British Library Cataloguing in Publication Information Available

Library of Congress Cataloging-in-Publication Data Available

ISBN 978-1-4758-2648-7 (cloth : alk. paper)
ISBN 978-1-4758-2651-7 (pbk. : alk. paper)
ISBN 978-1-4758-2652-4 (electronic)

∞ ™ The paper used in this publication meets the minimum requirements of American National Standard for Information Sciences Permanence of Paper for Printed Library Materials, ANSI/NISO Z39.48-1992.

Printed in the United States of America

For David and all God's children

Contents

Preface

Know Better, Do Better

I started my educational career as a kindergarten teacher in a large urban school district in central Illinois. Six months out of Illinois State University, I was hired three days before the start of the school year. Tyng Primary School, long since closed, served children in kindergarten through grade 4. Ninety-five percent of the students at the school lived in poverty.

On the first day of school, I was faced with fourteen kindergarten students—all of whom were African American. I quickly came to learn that the school had a mobility rate of 108 percent. By the time we were one month into the school year, I had thirty-one kindergarten students in my full-day kindergarten class, none of whom were in the original group of fourteen that I had on the first day.

As a first-year teacher with dreams and aspirations of making a difference for kids, I knew I needed to focus on reading. Unfortunately, even after graduating with honors from one of the leading teacher education programs in the state, I knew far too little about teaching children to read. I was assigned a mentor who, thankfully, demonstrated outstanding instructional methods in reading. With much study, practice, and trial and error, I gained the skills necessary to teach my students the alphabetic principle, phonemic awareness, and phonics.

Mostly out of sheer ignorance of the limitations my students were supposed to have because of their family backgrounds, I introduced my students to different kinds of literature. I engaged them in stories that were well beyond their independent reading levels to build their vocabulary and get them talking about literary elements.

Starting in September, I sent my students home with family homework related to the letters of the alphabet or the instructional theme of the month. The teachers with far more experience than I had quickly informed me that our students and parents could not be expected to do homework and return it to school. They told me, in no uncertain terms, that I was being naïve and that I would soon learn not to waste my time putting together family activities for my students. Thankfully, my students and their parents were as ignorant as I was about what could be expected of them.

That month, and every month thereafter, the students completed and returned their family homework. When it was time for parent-teacher conferences, my students' parents came to school and listened intently about their children's progress. Most of them were first-time kindergarten parents. They simply did not know that they were expected to be disengaged and unwilling to support their children's education. The families did what I asked of them and their children learned.

I certainly cannot claim that I was anything more than an adequate first-year teacher (although I was given an "excellent" evaluation rating because that's what principals did for all but the most inept new teachers). It took me most of the year to learn how to get 31 kindergarteners to walk in a straight, quiet line down the long hallway toward the cafeteria.

My first year of teaching was the first year that all schools in the state of Illinois were required to administer the Illinois Standards Achievement Test in reading and math. At the end of the year, I retained one student in kindergarten and turned over the other thirty students, in whom I had invested blood, sweat, and tears (literally) to get to read, to the first-grade team. I soon learned that only 21 percent of the third-graders at my school could read well enough to meet the standards of the ISAT. I was mortified and outraged. Again, I was apparently too ignorant of the way things worked in schools to know that I should not expect our students to meet the state standards.

During the next year, I not only taught kindergarten, but I also taught an after-school reading program for third- and fourth-graders. Still, I struggled with the realization that anything I did would only produce temporary results. At the end of each year, I would have to send my students to other grade levels where I would have no control over the instruction they would receive, the expectations that would be held for them, or the outcomes they would achieve.

Since that time, I have embarked on a quest to improve the educational outcomes of poor children, Latino children, and African American children. I have taught low-income kindergarteners and middle and upper class middle school students at a university laboratory school. I have been an assistant elementary principal, principal, assistant superintendent, and superintendent.

I have led professional development for schools and districts, presented at state and national conferences, and served as a consultant in a variety of schools. In all the schools I have visited, interacted with, and encountered, I have found poor African American children to be the lowest-achieving students. What is worse is that I have found that many educators are neither surprised nor dismayed by this fact.

Since the beginning of the accountability movement, the fact that a school serves low-income, African American, and Latino students has been the justification for dismally low achievement and school failure. Educators have spent so much energy on masking low achievement and manipulating test scores, proficiency rates, and other statistics that they have lost perspective of what success and achievement mean for our children. This loss of perspective is the essence of failure as a default—the pattern of attitudes, behaviors, structures, and decisions stemming from the belief that specific groups of students are likely to fail regardless of the actions of educators.

In my work in schools, I have repeatedly encountered failure as a default in many different settings. Often, those who have succumbed to the idea of failure as a default have done so unwittingly. In doing so, they have inadvertently helped to perpetuate the achievement gap in schools. This has been the case in schools that have set goals to close the achievement gap and in schools that have ignored the existence of a gap.

In 2012, I accepted a superintendency in a school district neighboring the school districts I attended while growing up in the Chicago suburbs and feeding into the high school I attended twenty years earlier. In school districts in the surrounding area, despite generally caring and dedicated staff members, I found a long history of structures, messages, and priorities within schools that communicated failure as a default. The sense that failure is a default for low-income, African American, and Latino children was just as pervasive in 2012 as it was when I graduated from high school despite the good intentions and hard work of teachers and leaders.

Inadvertently perpetuating the achievement gap is not necessarily about people not working hard. Sometimes it is about people working hard at doing what does not work. And sometimes it is about doing what works in a way that does not work for the children being served.

Mama used to say, "If you know better, you ought to do better." By examining the phenomenon of failure as a default in our schools, we can identify and change the ways in which schools inadvertently perpetuate the achievement gap. This book is for educators and leaders at all levels who are willing to examine their practice, challenge the status quo, and work intentionally to end failure as a default in schools and achieve success for all of our children.

Acknowledgments

This book represents over twenty years of experiences in many different schools and districts. I would like to thank all of those who have entrusted me with the education of their children as well as the many educators and school leaders who have allowed me to observe, interact with, and learn from them. I would also like to thank the children through the years who have frustrated and inspired me, tugged at my heartstrings, kept me awake at night, and driven everything I do as an educator and leader.

I would also like to thank my colleague, Mr. Ricardo Aceves, for reading and commenting on the manuscript. Rick is an outstanding educator, whose insight and commitment to educating all children is a continual comfort and inspiration to me. Finally, I would like to thank my husband and greatest supporter, Bishop A. Q. Hill, and my pride and joy, my son and future doctor, David.

Introduction

No Fault Default

"Where there is no vision, the people perish."

—Proverbs 29:18, KJV

This truth describes the plight that can be found in many school districts serving African American students, Latino students, and students living in poverty. The visions of success that may have once existed among educators and leaders have been obscured by years of persistent failure (made even more public by No Child Left Behind [NCLB] and the school reform movement), generations of poverty, and decades of educational neglect. Without a true vision of success, it is easy to confuse mediocrity with success. In my experiences as a parent, educator, and school leader, I have witnessed this phenomenon in education many times.

Broad-based educational reform efforts grounded in legislating educational opportunity have largely served to immerse the education profession more fully into an achievement gap ideology that is pervasive in American society. The result is a system of schooling that is operated and led by a multigenerational cohort that has been indoctrinated with the belief that failure is a default for some children.

Educators, school leaders, teacher educators, and policy makers have heard much about the persistent achievement gap (i.e., the significant difference in test score achievement, grades, and educational attainment between African American students, Latino students, and white students and between middle class students and students living in poverty). Talk of the achievement gap has subsumed our school-reform discussions, particularly since the passage of NCLB.

In 2000, when the NCLB Act began, the law enjoyed bipartisan support in Congress. Politics makes strange bedfellows. Liberals supported the law to address the persistent achievement gap and the inequities in funding, resources, and teacher quality among schools. Conservatives supported the law because of its support of school choice and emphasis on empowering parents.

The unique combination of the liberal focus on collective responsibility and understanding poverty and the conservative focus on personal responsibility and meritocracy yielded a law that required annual standardized testing in reading, math, and science; the disaggregation of student achievement data; the hiring of "highly qualified" (HQ) teachers for all students; and schools and districts achieving "Adequate Yearly Progress" (AYP) in raising the percentage of students identified as proficient based on the standardized tests from year to year.

In addition, the law required schools to meet "Annual Measurable Achievement Objectives" (AMAO) for students with limited English proficiency. AMAO required growth in both academic and English proficiency for English language learners. Like academic proficiency, English proficiency was to be measured through the use of standardized tests.

By requiring achievement data to be disaggregated, liberal leaders prevented schools from being able to escape accountability by hiding behind overall scores. Schools with many high-achieving students would now have to pay attention to the smaller groups of students who were achieving at lower levels (e.g., African American students, Latino students, English language learners, students with disabilities, low-income students, etc.). Schools and districts would be held accountable for the achievement and continual growth of every identifiable "subgroup"[1] in the school.

By requiring annual standardized testing, leaders shined a spotlight on proficiency levels (far too many of which were dismally low) at public schools throughout the United States. Political and civil rights leaders took advantage of the sense of urgency and crisis created by the poor state of affairs in too many schools.

Since the passage of the No Child Left Behind Act, the quest to close the achievement gap in ways that would allow districts and schools to make AYP and AMAO on state tests has resulted in schools' implementing questionable or downright detrimental practices, such as providing tutoring services only to the "bubble kids,"[2] devoting weeks of instruction to test-prep activities, categorizing students as those who "count" and those who "do not count," rapidly moving students from their native language to English only,[3] and eliminating recess (and art, and music, and physical education) to gain more time to prepare for tests.

Much has been said and written about the achievement gap, but we as educators and as a society have done very little to confront or eradicate the ideology that perpetuates the poor outcomes for certain groups of students. The achievement gap ideology is characterized by a specific set of widely held attitudes or beliefs about the qualities, value, and abilities of different groups that undergird educational, economic, and social inequality.[4]

Fifteen years of No Child Left Behind has shown us what happens when we try to legislate a change in outcomes without creating a change in beliefs. When individuals value statistics over children and believe authentic success is impossible or improbable for the people they serve, they are far more likely to disregard the needs of children in their efforts to produce the statistical outcomes that are required.

It is nearly impossible to directly change long-standing beliefs. Instead, educators can change people's behaviors and experiences. As people have experiences that contradict their beliefs, they can modify their belief structures accordingly. Those who are unwilling or unable to adapt to a reality in which all children are capable of and expected to achieve success do not belong in our schools.

Throughout this book, I use the phrase "failure as a default" to describe an attitude and belief system in which it is assumed that specific groups of children, specific schools, and specific individuals (e.g., those who are African American, Latino, low income, disabled, urban, at risk, etc.) will fail. This assumption leads to a general lack of concern, urgency, or willingness to change our actions when failure is anticipated.

I use the word "default" in its computer science definition (although other definitions also apply, as we will see later). Default is a noun defined as "a value that a program or operating system assumes, or a course of action that a program or operating system will take, when the user or programmer specifies no overriding value or action" (Dictionary.com). An educational definition of "default" that I use throughout this book is an outcome that is assumed, expected, and accepted as a matter of course or a path that individuals or events are expected to take when no exceptional or heroic measures are taken to override the anticipated outcome.

Defaults are built into every system. These defaults, whether structural or psychological, help people know what to expect in a normal situation. If people feel that change is happening too rapidly or that changes have moved them too far from the accepted way of doing things, they always have the option (and the tendency) to reset to the default. Unless we go into the system and change the default settings, they will always be inherent in the organization even if we make wholesale changes to the way we do things. Programs and organizations are designed to operate based on defaults.

The problem with school reform is that schools were initially designed to produce the outcomes they are currently producing. Our schools are not failing. They are succeeding at their original purpose. The default for our school system is producing a small number of liberally and classically educated leaders, a larger number of competent managers, a still larger number of compliant workers, and a set of menial laborers who will not aspire to anything else.

Anyone who cannot fit into these categories is ushered out of the system as early as possible to avoid wasting resources. Moreover, the expectation that students are sorted into groups based on their demographics (i.e., gender, race, nationality) and the socioeconomic and cultural background and status of their families is a default in US schools.

Even with the significant changes that have impacted schooling—movement to a factory model of education, increasing education of girls, creation of the comprehensive high school, racial integration, and the standards and accountability movement—the defaults that are built into the system have remained intact. As a result, the pattern of outcomes has not changed over time.

As opposed to focusing on the differences in outcomes and achievement, in recent years, the term "opportunity gap" has been used in achievement gap discussions. The use of "opportunity gap" shifts the focus from the differences in outcomes to the differences in opportunity. This way of thinking appeases those who feel as though it is not the responsibility of schools to produce equal outcomes. Instead, schools should only be expected to offer equal opportunities.

A positive aspect of this approach is that it supports the idea that African American students, Latino students, and poor students are not inherently less capable than white, native English–speaking, middle class students. Focusing on equalizing opportunities is a palatable way to address inequitable resources and treatment. It also promotes the idea of personal responsibility.

However, the focus on eliminating the opportunity gap negates schools' accountability for outcomes. If student achievement is low, it can simply be attributed to students' not taking advantage of the opportunities presented. As we examine failure as a default, we will note ways that failure as a default controverts opportunities that are made available.

This book explores and combats the belief that serves as the linchpin for the achievement gap ideology—failure as a default. It provides readers with concrete actions needed to eradicate all evidence of this belief system in schools and districts. This book is organized into two parts. Part 1, Every Good-Bye Ain't Gone, focuses on the origin, signs, and symptoms of failure as a default in American schools. Chapter 1 chronicles the evidence of failure as a default in educational policy, popular media, and academia. Chapter 2 traces the achievement gap ideology of failure as a default through the era of public school accountability.

Chapter 3 examines the signs and symptoms of failure as a default in individual public schools and school districts. Educational leaders and policy makers will be able to determine the extent to which failure as a default impacts their systems. Chapter 4 presents a new vision to calibrate our definition of quality education for African American, Latino, and low-income students in America's public schools.

Part II, A Long Time Coming, presents educational leaders and policy makers with the keys to eradicate failure as a default from public schools and public school districts. Chapter 5 discusses ways to change the structures within school districts that promote and perpetuate failure as a default. Chapter 6 focuses on the messages sent to, from, and within school districts. Chapter 7 examines educator and school leader attitudes and behaviors that perpetuate the achievement gap. Chapter 8 is a special message for educational policy makers, legislators, and other leaders.

In each of these chapters, readers will learn to identify failure as a default in school district structures, messages, attitudes, and behaviors. Readers will then examine specific ways to counteract the past and make purposeful changes for the future. The book concludes with a discussion of the potency and efficacy of educational leaders and policy makers in creating and sustaining a culture of authentic success for all children.

This book is based on some basic assumptions. First, all children have the capacity for authentic success in school and in life. Second, although the purpose of schooling has changed over time, the purpose of today's schools must be to provide all children with the best possible preparation for their future roles as workers, leaders, citizens, and visionaries. Third, education is a noble and life-shaping profession that, more often than not, is chosen by individuals who love children and have an overwhelming desire to witness and be a part of their growth and success.

The assumption that all children have the capacity for success seems very simple, but this simple belief is a requirement for combating the achievement gap. Along with this belief in children's capacity to learn and succeed goes the coinciding belief that educators cannot predict the heights or limits of a child's learning and success. The educator's role is to teach, support, challenge, and inspire all children to reach, exceed, and extend the limits of their capacity.

Schools can no longer serve the purpose of sorting students for levels of achievement based on demographics. In a society in which over 50 percent of elementary school students are low income and most students are African American, Latino, or other ethnic/racial "minorities," our nation simply cannot afford to accept the failure of "nonwhite," non–middle class children in our schools. This will necessitate a significant change in our collective understanding of the purpose of schools. We must both confront and change our collective view of what schools are designed to do.

Teachers, educational leaders, and educators of all kinds care about students. The vast majority simply want to do their jobs and do them well. The problem of the achievement gap and the idea of failure as a default did not originate from educators. They are not at fault for the many ways in which schools help perpetuate the achievement gap. Simply holding teachers accountable, evaluating them based on test scores, eliminating the "bad apples," or tying their wages to high-stakes tests will not eliminate the achievement gap or rid our schools or society of the idea of failure as a default.

Teachers and school leaders are not to blame, but as is explored throughout this book, they have tremendous power to change the experiences of our students in schools. With that power comes the immense responsibility of creating or re-creating our schools as places where all children can learn.

Throughout this book, I refer repeatedly to the ways in which schools inadvertently perpetuate the achievement gap. This can happen by actively making decisions that work against students, by passively ignoring conditions that are detrimental to students, or by neglecting actions that could help students.

I do not believe that schools are the sole creators of or contributors to the achievement gap. However, I do believe that it is our responsibility as educators, leaders, and policy makers to ensure that we do what we know, what research tells us, what experience has taught us, and what communities have shared with us is right by all of our children. Until we create schools in which we do not exacerbate the disadvantages faced by some of our students, we cannot simply blame the achievement gap on outside factors.

The examples and vignettes in this book are gleaned from real students, communities, schools, and districts.[5] They are shared to help educators and policy makers develop an understanding of what failure as a default means to individuals and families and, in turn, to local schools, communities, and our nation. Student by student, educator by educator, class by class, school by school, community by community, and state by state, we can combat the achievement gap by ending failure as a default and creating schools that provide pathways to success for every child.

NOTES

1. As a part of each state's plan to implement the law, each state had to set the number of students in a school or district that would constitute an identifiable subgroup. In Illinois, the number was 45. Schools with fewer than 45 African American students, English language learners, etc., were not held accountable for the performance of these subgroups. Because the subgroup size was a number instead of a percentage, small schools would not be responsible for any subgroups, whereas large schools could have all of them.

2. Students who score just a few points below the cut score on high-stakes tests are labeled bubble kids. Schools often target programs/services to these students to make rapid gains in proficiency rates with minimal investment.

3. A great reference for learning about the impact of moving students to English while neglecting their native language is *Subtractive Schooling* by Angela Valenzuela.

4. For a full discussion of the achievement gap ideology, see *Every Closed Eye Ain't Sleep: African American Perspectives on the Achievement Gap* by Teresa D. Hill.

5. Details have been modified or omitted to preserve confidentiality.

I

Every Good-Bye Ain't Gone

Chapter One

The Ideology of Inequality

"We hold these truths to be self-evident, that all men are created equal."
—Jefferson, 1776 (from the Declaration of Independence)

"Comparing them by their faculties of memory, reason, and imagination, it appears to me, that in memory they are equal to the whites; in reason much inferior, as I think one could scarcely be found capable of tracing and comprehending the investigations of Euclid; and that in imagination they are dull, tasteless, and anomalous."
—Jefferson, 1785 (as cited in Jordan 1969)

A belief in racial inequality is a fundamental part of the United States of America. The same founding father who penned the phrase "all men are created equal" argued vehemently that African Americans were inferior to whites—a belief he supported with conclusions he drew from his experiences as a holder of enslaved African Americans. These seemingly diametrically opposed beliefs provide an example of the pervasiveness of the American societal belief in inequality despite the American ideal of equality.

Thomas Jefferson was one of many who argued the intellectual limitations of both enslaved and free African Americans. He wrote about many of the stereotypes of African American inferiority that persist in white supremacy circles today.

In Jefferson's view, African Americans did not need as much sleep; were "ardent for their women" but without tenderness of real love, overly sensual and focused on pleasure, less affected by loss and heartache, and prone to laziness when not forced to work; and lacked higher-level intellect and creativity (Jordan 1969). Beliefs such as these, as well as similar beliefs about Native Americans, Latinos, and other "nonwhite"[1] ethnic groups, have been passed down through the generations and embedded in the foundations of American society.

Over 200 years later, overtly racist beliefs and statements are shunned in polite society. However, the idea of the achievement gap (i.e., the difference in academic achievement and outcomes among racial, ethnic, and socioeconomic groups) is part of the national consciousness. Educators, educational leaders, policy makers, parents, and those with no connection to schools recognize the term "achievement gap." More importantly, each of these groups recognizes and accepts the idea that some groups routinely demonstrate lower achievement and attainment in schools (and in life) when compared to white middle class children.

Each of these groups has also largely subscribed to the false dichotomy that places white middle class children in contrast to all others. The idea that white middle class children are the standard to which all others are to be compared has been accepted without much question. This phenomenon is seen in media reports and even in educational research in which groups of children are routinely referred to as "white" and "nonwhite" or as "white" and "minority."

The term "nonwhite" includes African American, Latino, Native American, and Asian students as well as immigrant children who are identified with any of these groups. The term "minority" is typically reserved for ethnic groups stemming from outside of Europe.

The frequent refrain of these reports is that "nonwhites" and "minorities" perform differently than "whites." Specifically, African American, Latino, and Native American children underperform their white peers. Asian students, on the other hand, outperform white students (particularly in math and science).

The idea of the achievement gap is pervasive when applied to both schools and other aspects of American society. Evidence of this can be seen throughout the media messages about and coverage of schools, testing, student achievement, poverty, and racial issues.

One type of media message about the achievement gap is the confirmation story. These stories serve as confirmation or proof of the underachievement of African American and Latino communities as well as poor communities. On September 24, 2015, *US News & World Report* published an article titled "Study Finds Students Underperform in Schools with Large Black Populations" (Camera 2015). The article presented the results of a study conducted by the National Center for Educational Statistics that concluded that both African American and white students performed worse on standardized tests if they went to schools with 40 percent or more African American students.

On September 14, 2015, the *Los Angeles Times* published another example of a confirmation story. The article titled "Achievement Gaps Widen for California's Black and Latino Students" shared information from the results of new California statewide tests based on higher "college and career ready" standards (Blume 2015). The focus of the story was that "although scores declined for all students, blacks and Latinos saw significantly greater drops than whites and Asians, widening the already large gap that was evident in results from earlier years."

Other confirmation headlines abound, such as "Despite Advances, Racial Achievement Gap Widens" (Ostashevsky 2016), "Achievement Gap Between White and Black Students Still Gaping" (Camera 2016), "Education Gap Grows Between Rich and Poor, Studies Show" (Tavernise 2012), "Gains in Reading for Hispanic Students Overshadowed by Achievement Gaps" (Camera 2016).

Media messages confirming the existence of the achievement gap can be seen in the media in cities and towns throughout the nation. The NCLB requirement to disaggregate and publicly release test score information has made stories about the persistent achievement gap an annual ritual.

Another type of message about the gap is the progress story. These stories demonstrate that progress is being made while also highlighting the idea that even these heroic efforts do not eliminate the gap. These stories may also have the effect of normalizing student underachievement for certain students. One such story appearing in the *San Francisco Chronicle* on August 24, 2016 (Tucker 2016), had the headline "Good News on School Test Scores Can't Disguise Achievement Gap."

The story highlighted the improvement in standardized test scores for the San Francisco, California, school district but also demonstrated that even this improvement in scores did not shrink the achievement gap. The reporter noted how a new reading and language arts curriculum had created significant improvement in student achievement. The writer then went on to explain that the district has the largest achievement gap in the state.

Media messages about the achievement gap also include the exception story. In these stories, one individual or school has "beaten the odds" and achieved a level of success beyond that which was predicted. Examples of these exception stories can often be found in stories about standout schools or charismatic leaders. One example of an exception story is "Urban Prep School in Chicago Boasts 100 Percent College Acceptance Rate, 7th Year in a Row" (Kinney 2016). This media story, and many others like it, highlights the success of Urban Prep, a public charter high school for boys in Chicago. Each year for the past seven years, all graduates of Urban Prep have been admitted to four-year colleges or universities.

Other exception stories have focused on the accomplishments of Geoffrey Canada and the Harlem Children's Zone. These stories take the focus off the system and place it instead on the individual school or leader, thereby supporting the concept of meritocracy.

THE ACHIEVEMENT GAP IDEOLOGY

Our collective knowledge of and beliefs about the achievement gap can best be described as an ideology. An ideology is defined as "a systematic body of concepts especially about human life and culture" that includes "integrated assertions, theories and aims that constitute a sociopolitical program" (Dictionary.com). The achievement gap ideology is a systematic integrated set of beliefs that permeate American society.

Grounded in America's history of slavery, racism, classism, and cultural protectionism, the achievement gap ideology incorporates several beliefs that are inherent to American culture (Hill 2011). The first of these beliefs is that there are authentic, fundamental differences between people of different races, classes, and cultures and that these differences impact achievement in school and life. Specifically, African American, Latino, and poor people are less able to achieve in schools and life.

A fundamental component of a belief in race as a biological reality is the corresponding belief that there are certain immutable qualities that are associated with members of each race. Some racial beliefs are relatively benign, while others form the basis of white supremacist and other racist beliefs. Whether malicious or benign, racial beliefs impact the interactions among individuals and groups.

Positive and negative racial beliefs and stereotypes are pervasive in literature and media. For example, the racial beliefs/stereotypes about African

American people include that they are physically strong, verbally and physically aggressive, hypersexual, highly tolerant of pain, athletic, of low intelligence, musically/rhythmically talented, loud and large. In schools, this translates to African American children being judged as scary, hard to discipline, and intimidating. These perceptions carry over into the larger society and impact community interaction—most notably interactions between members of the African American community and law enforcement officers in some communities.

Meanwhile, Latino people are typically lumped into one group without regard to their country or region of ancestry. Latino people are stereotyped as highly religious, "hot headed," misogynistic, lower class, uneducated, non–English speaking, industrious, and good with their hands, while also being lazy. This translates into Latino children being judged as incommunicative, devious if speaking Spanish, intimidating when angry (if male), meek and docile (if female), and not focused on education.

The prevalent racial beliefs/stereotypes regarding Asian people (who, like Latino people, are lumped together regardless of their country of ancestry) characterize them as small, physically weak, highly intelligent, compliant, devious, unemotional, and particularly good at math and science. The result is that Asian children are seen as ideal students who require little attention.

Even people who are identified as white cannot escape the racial belief structure. White people are characterized as wholesome, intelligent, entrepreneurial, American, "red blooded" (when male), and "white bread and mayonnaise." For white students, the result is that white students are seen as normal and the structure of schools is designed for them. Each of these stereotypes and assumptions and many others constitute part of the achievement gap ideology. Developing an understanding of the biases and stereotypes is important because they impact the interactions of individuals and groups.

The second belief that makes up the achievement gap ideology is that educators, psychologists, and others can both measure and predict individual intelligence and potential. Key to this belief is the fact that those in power define what is valued as intelligence and potential. The purported measurement of intelligence has a long history. Beginning with the development of the first IQ tests in the early 1900s, the results of these tests have been used to both sort individuals based on their supposed potential and to provide evidence of the assumed inferiority of African Americans and other "non-white" ethnic groups.[2]

The first intelligence test was developed by Alfred Binet and was soon promoted by Henry Herbert Goddard to identify children who were "feeble-minded" and, thus, incapable of learning in a school setting (Benjamin 2009). Less than a decade later, a new version of the intelligence test that could be administered to large groups was developed for the US Army. The sole purpose of the test was to sort the thousands of newly drafted soldiers into groups that could be assigned to different roles. Eugenicists embraced the idea of measuring intelligence as a way to identify those who should breed and those who should be prevented from procreating.

These tests began to be used widely in schools after the first administration of the Scholastic Aptitude Test in 1926 (Fletcher 2009). The use of intelligence tests in school brought about widespread acceptance of a definition of intelligence that was based on white middle and upper class children. Many years later, that definition of intelligence, the belief that it can be measured and predicted, and the urge to make decisions based on the results of aptitude measurement continue to prevail in the current use of standardized tests.

A third element of the achievement gap ideology is the idea that sorting students and educating them according to their potential is a core role of schools. This sorting takes place both within and among schools. The kind of education provided to students is determined based on the students' perceived or projected role and status in society.

Children from upper class families are expected to be future leaders and managers. Their coursework and day-to-day experiences in schools support the realization of this expectation. Children from families in poverty are expected to become compliant workers and consumers, and this expectation is supported by their schooling as well.

At Barrington High School in Barrington, Illinois, a wealthy northern suburb of Chicago, the available coursework includes thirty-four Advanced Placement (AP) courses, including four different AP Physics courses and three AP Studio Art courses; electives such as Mobile App Development, Digital Web Design, and Photojournalism; and world language courses in five languages—French, German, Spanish, Mandarin Chinese, and Latin (www.barrington220.org 2016). The students there have access to all the courses and programs necessary to make them comfortable in prestigious universities, wealthy communities, and leadership roles.

At Morgan Park High School in a low-income area on the south side of Chicago, Illinois, the available coursework includes no Advanced Placement

(AP) classes, two languages—French and Spanish—and a few International Baccalaureate (IB) classes (www.morganparkcps.org 2016). Student choices are limited. When the students from Morgan Park arrive at a university, they do not have as many of the experiences necessary to prepare them to be comfortable interacting with others. This same comparison can be made between middle schools and high schools in many different areas.

The differences between schools in different communities illustrate the sorting process between schools. However, the sorting process also takes place within schools. Within a single high school or middle school, there are numerous structures that support the sorting of students. The long-standing practice of tracking (i.e., assigning students to different courses and/or different levels of courses based on perceived ability) allows students attending the same school to experience completely different coursework and day-to-day experiences. Gifted programs, special education programs, and remedial programs also create structures for sorting students.

Palpable differences also exist in the treatment of and communication with students in wealthy and low-income schools and communities. Research has shown the vast differences in the communication styles school staff members use with low-income and middle and upper class parents (Lott 2001). These differences in interaction often extend to students.

Students from families in poverty are treated differently than middle class and wealthy students, who are expected to become managers and leaders. Middle class and wealthy students are routinely provided more choice and autonomy throughout their educational experiences. Interactions with these students are typically characterized by free expression of ideas, discussions about reasons for decisions, acceptance of dissent and debate, and student decision making.

On the other hand, low-income students are given more directives, more rules and parameters, and more limits. Interactions with low-income, African American, and Latino students are often characterized by rote questions and answers, little student-directed talk, and many teacher directives. Student decision making is often limited by school and classroom structures, and student dissent and debate is frowned upon.

The fourth element of the achievement gap ideology is the belief that specific values are "right" and that those who do not espouse those values are immoral or inferior. This ties to the idea that white middle class individuals represent the norm. White middle class values are the mainstream. Perceived or actual lack of adherence to mainstream values is seen as indicative of a lack of values.

The focus on white middle class values has been particularly strong throughout the last few decades as the United States has been embroiled in what has been termed the "culture wars." This has included a focus on the "traditional" family, defined as a nuclear family with two parents (one male and one female) with traditional gender roles.

It has also included a strong focus on the idea of meritocracy in which some individuals have more and achieve more because they deserve more or have earned more. In this view, children rightly benefit from the efforts of their parents. A child who is born into a middle class or upper class family deserves the benefits he or she receives from the circumstances of his/her birth because of the efforts of the child's parents.

Mainstream values also include an expectation of compliance with authority, wholesomeness, patriarchy, the exaltation of masculinity, and a general acceptance of Christianity as the undergirding of American values. Communities and families that do not adhere to these values are considered to be inferior. Those who advocate opposing viewpoints are seen as a threat to the wholesome "family values" on which the nation was built.

Failure as a Default

The final belief that makes up the achievement gap ideology is the belief that failure is a default for some people. This part of the achievement gap ideology, more than any other, impacts the way schools are structured and educators interact with students and their families. It also impacts the way policy makers and leaders think about schooling.

A default is an outcome that is assumed, expected, and accepted as a matter of course, or a path that individuals or events are expected to take when no exceptional or heroic measures are taken to override the anticipated outcome. The idea that African American students, Latino students, and students in poverty routinely underperform white middle class children and that this underachievement is to be expected regardless of the practices of educators is the essence of failure as a default in schools.

When failure is the default, poor outcomes are accepted as "the way things are." This results in little urgency to change outcomes (urgency). A lack of urgency causes other concerns to be prioritized over student outcomes. In addition, when failure is a default, individuals in the system have little faith or confidence that anything they do will be effective in changing the outcome (efficacy). This lack of efficacy is a powerful deterrent to meaningful effort. And when failure is the default, people lack the collective knowledge, experience, and expertise to create an outcome of success (capacity). The dearth of capacity helps to restart the cycle.

Educators do not have the capacity to meet student needs and achieve positive outcomes. Therefore, generations of students fail. Generations of educators are immersed in African American, Latino, and poor student failure and feel no urgency to change conditions that they believe have always existed. Without either the capacity or urgency to change practices, and faced with a long history of messages of failure, educators have little reason to believe in their ability to create success. Policy makers and families are also impacted by this failure as a default cycle.

One of the most frustrating aspects of the achievement gap for educators is the idea that an achievement gap remains because educators do not care, they are lazy, or they harbor hatred against certain groups of children. This kind of thinking leads to myriad reforms designed to fix, punish, coerce, cajole, or eliminate educators, thereby combating the achievement gap. Like the vast majority of families, the vast majority of educators care deeply about their students and have an authentic desire to do what is best for them. They also have limits, weaknesses, and biases.

Educators, policy makers, and to a lesser extent, families have been immersed in the achievement gap ideology and the idea of failure as a default. Today's educators were educated in schools in which the achievement gap was just a matter of fact. The Generation Xers were the subject of studies and the catalyst for *A Nation at Risk*. The Millennials came of age under the regime of the No Child Left Behind Act. The previous generation, the Baby Boomers, attended segregated schools and newly desegregated schools. The same applies to today's educational policy makers. These experiences color the way we do school.

In addition, the structure of schools in the United States has changed little since the Industrial Revolution. The structures that were put in place in the early 1900s based on the achievement gap ideology remain in place in schools today. Thus, schools create the outcomes they were designed to produce. Schools produce a small number of future leaders, a larger number of professionals and managers, and even more compliant workers. Students who do not fit into one of these categories often are steered toward menial labor or ushered out of the school system completely.

As in the past, the class of future leaders is more likely to include white upper class children who come from families of privilege. The class of future managers and professionals (including educators) is likely to include mostly white middle class children and a small number of middle class children from other backgrounds whose families occupy the same class. The compliant worker class typically includes poor and working class white children and working class and middle class African American and Latino students. The class of menial laborers often includes poor children of all races.

Without addressing the structures inherent in the United States' system of schooling, these structures will continue to shape the outcomes for children. School reforms, such as closing schools, tying teacher pay to test scores, eliminating teacher tenure, and implementing school "turnarounds," may have their place in educational policy, but they will not eliminate the achievement gap within or across schools.

When failure is a default, educators, policy makers, and leaders without the urgency, efficacy, or capacity to make meaningful change instead make decisions and replicate structures that serve only to reinforce and perpetuate the achievement gap. To combat the achievement gap, educators, policy makers, and educational leaders must understand, confront, and systematically eradicate the belief system that perpetuates it—failure as a default.

NOTES

1. "White" is not a racial descriptor. It is a social construct that has had changes to its definition over time. For example, at one time the Irish did not receive the privilege of being considered "white." For an in-depth discussion of the social construction of race, consider consulting *The Race Myth: Why We Pretend Race Exists in America* by Joseph L. Graves Jr. (Penguin Group, 2004).

2. At the time of the development of the first IQ tests, "nonwhite" notably included individuals who were Irish as well as those who were Italian.

Chapter Two

Failure and Accountability

"If an unfriendly foreign power had attempted to impose on America the mediocre educational performance that exists today, we might well have viewed it as an act of war. As it stands, we have allowed this to happen to ourselves."

—*A Nation at Risk* (National Commission on Excellence in Education 1983, 1)

The idea of failure as a default has influenced and been influenced by the ebb and flow of the American narrative of educational failure and accountability. The history of school accountability and educational reform sheds light on the current state of educational policy. The specific focus on the achievement gap and educational inequality has come and gone multiple times in the recent history of public schools.

The narrative of the achievement gap in American schools is closely intertwined with the tale of school reform. The close relationship between the narrative of the achievement gap and the progress of school reform is, perhaps, best illustrated by considering the education of African American children since, through most of the twentieth century, the achievement gap was routinely referred to as the "black-white" achievement gap.

Although there was much debate about the education of African American youth prior to desegregation, there was little concern about what we now know as the achievement gap. It was accepted that African American children would not be educated to the same level as white middle class children. Educational inequality based on race was accepted as a matter of course. It was assumed that African American children and white children were being educated to fulfill different roles and to inhabit different classes in society. As a result, there was no need for African American children to receive the same kind or quality of education as white children.

The difference in the quality of education received by African American children compared to white children was a key argument in the *Brown v. Board of Education* case. Thurgood Marshall's argument focused not only on children's educational opportunities in schools, but also on the social and economic purposes of schooling (Brown v. Board of Education 1954). He argued that the experiences of students in schools and their access to social connections were critical to equality in public schools.

His arguments led the Supreme Court to determine that the segregated schools were "inherently unequal." This determination was made based in part on the successful argument that forcing African American students to attend segregated schools created a social stigma that could only be expected to negatively impact African American children.

It was not until schools were desegregated that the term "achievement gap" began to be used in educational circles. Even then, the source of the achievement gap was not seen as a result of anything that took place in school. Rather, the achievement gap analyzed the result of deficiencies in African American children and their families and communities.

When schools began to be desegregated throughout the United States, the schools serving African American children were often closed. The African American teachers and school leaders were dismissed, and African American students were integrated into schools with white students, white teachers, and white leaders. Segregation continued within the walls of the integrated schools through structures that continue to exist today—tracking, detention, and in-school suspension and social isolation.

In 1965, Daniel Patrick Moynihan released a report on the African American family. The report, titled "The Negro Family: The Case for National Action," identified numerous familial and cultural conditions stemming from years of slavery and racism that Moynihan identified as the source of the destruction of black families and the underachievement of African American children (Moynihan 1965).

Moynihan made the case that underachievement resulted from conditions within the African American community. In his view, the breakdown of the family was the source of the poor condition of African Americans in the United States. Schools and educational inequality were not even considered factors in the report.

Researchers in the 1960s correctly argued that poverty had a significant negative effect on student achievement in schools. The Civil Rights Act of 1964 included a commission for a survey and study of educational opportunity in the United States. In the resulting report "Equality of Educational Opportunity" also known as the "Coleman Report," sociologist James Coleman took the research to the next step by considering the conditions and social and economic factors within and around schools (Coleman 1966).

In the first study of its kind, and the last study to look at schools so comprehensively, Coleman clearly identified the differences in conditions and resources in schools that served different populations of students and discussed the impact that this was likely to have on student and community outcomes. He argued that policy makers and researchers should not only consider educational inputs as educational opportunity but should also consider equality of outcomes.

The Coleman Report identified disparities in school funding, teacher preparation, and curriculum. It also shed light on the continuing segregation of schools in the United States as well as the differences in student achievement and community achievement outcomes as measured by the standardized tests and other statistics of the time. The report even included information about practices that exacerbated segregation, such as tracking and exclusionary discipline.

Also included in Coleman's research were the results of numerous surveys, interviews, and other research on other factors impacting the relative performance of students of different racial, ethnic, and socioeconomic backgrounds. These are the results for which the Coleman Report became best known.

By the time Ronald Reagan took office in 1981, what was termed the "black-white achievement gap" had been decreasing slowly but steadily. However, Reagan's take on education was different than that of his predecessors. Ronald Reagan commissioned a study of the quality of America's public schools. The study shifted the focus from considering family, community, and economic dynamics as sources of underachievement to placing the responsibility for lackluster achievement squarely on the shoulders of schools and educators. It made improving achievement in schools an imperative for society.

The resulting report, titled *A Nation at Risk*, set off a new public school reform movement characterized by a sense of panic and danger. The report begins with the statement, "We report to the American people that while we can take justifiable pride in what our schools and colleges have historically accomplished and contributed to the United States and the well-being of its people, the educational foundations of our society are presently being eroded by a rising tide of mediocrity that *threatens our very future as a Nation and a people*" [emphasis added] (National Commission on Excellence in Education 1983, 1).

In addition to characterizing the education system (and, by extension, the educators who run it) as a national threat, one of the many impacts of *A Nation at Risk* was a shift in focus from equity for African American students and poor students in schools to overall student achievement. The writers specifically addressed the concern for equity and explained the rationale for their focus on achievement by stating:

> We do not believe that a public commitment to excellence and educational reform must be made at the expense of a strong public commitment to the equitable treatment of our diverse population. The twin goals of equity and high-quality schooling have profound and practical meaning for our economy and society, and we cannot permit one to yield to the other either in principle or in practice. To do so would deny young people their chance to learn and live according to their aspirations and abilities. It also would lead to a generalized accommodation to mediocrity in our society on the one hand or the creation of an undemocratic elitism on the other. (National Commission on Excellence in Education 1983, 4)

It is important to note that the report refers to "equitable treatment," not equitable programs, services, resources, or achievement. Unlike the Coleman Report, *A Nation at Risk* argued for neither equitable inputs nor equal outcomes.

While expressing the value of equitable treatment, the writers were careful to focus on children having a *"chance to learn* and live according to their *aspirations and abilities* [emphases added]" (ibid. 1983). This reflected a focus on personal responsibility that was a hallmark of the conservative approach to the achievement gap. It also assumed and supported the common practice of basing educational decisions on students' perceived abilities.

The report not only shifted the focus from equity but also indicted the practice of making schools responsible for programs and structures to meet students' nonacademic needs. *A Nation at Risk* steered policy away from the Moynihan Report and the Coleman Report. Instead of advocating educational practices to combat the disadvantages identified by Moynihan and Coleman, *A Nation at Risk* minimized these factors and focused on school-based factors that the commission categorized as Content, Expectations, Time, and Teaching.

In the category of Content, the commission took exception to the move toward the "general track," instead advocating for maintaining a vocational track and a college preparatory track. They pointed out that, in their opinion, students were offered too much choice of curriculum options and too many courses outside of the "core" curriculum.

Expectations were addressed in a variety of ways in both the Coleman Report and the Moynihan Report. However, *A Nation at Risk* defined expectations as the amount of work required to obtain a high school diploma and enter and complete college. Specifically, the commission took issue with "minimum competency" high school electives. They concluded that there was too little homework, too few math and science requirements, textbooks that were too easy, and too many colleges that accepted all applicants.

A Nation at Risk labeled English, math, science, and social studies as the "New Basics." The commission urged a focus on raising student achievement in the new basics as a way to steer America away from educational mediocrity and toward excellence.

The shift in focus away from equity was the start of a thirty-year stagnation in the achievement gap. Not only has the gap persisted and grown between African American children and white children, but it has also grown between middle class children and children living in poverty. As the numbers of Latino students have increased in American schools, their lower relative performance in schools has also been highlighted.

On March 31, 1994, President Bill Clinton signed a set of broad goals and specific policies known as the Goals 2000: Educate America Act (H.R. 1804 1994). These goals became the basis for what was to become the standards and accountability movement. Goals 2000 did not in any way contradict the recommendations of *A Nation at Risk*. Instead, it codified the thinking upon which the report was based into law and initiated policy prescriptions that continue to have a strong impact on public education policy. By setting several measurable outcome-based goals, the law set the stage for the current reliance on high-stakes testing to ensure educator accountability.

Goals 2000 identified eight goals. They included School Readiness; School Completion; Student Achievement and Citizenship; Teacher Education and Professional Development; Mathematics and Science; Adult Literacy and Lifelong Learning; Safe, Disciplined, and Alcohol- and Drug-Free

Schools; and Parental Participation. Each of these goals was written beginning with "by the year 2000" and ending with a goal for every student, every school, all children, or the nation's teaching force.

Influenced by civil rights leaders and the liberal belief in collective responsibility, Goals 2000 incorporated a renewed interest in equitable outcomes for African American students, Latino students, and students in poverty. Two of the eight Goals 2000 educational goals included objectives specifically designed to address the achievement gap. These included a School Completion goal aimed at reducing the dropout rate, and the Math and Science goal aimed at increase America's standing in those two disciplines. In addition, all the goals were stated with a focus on all children.

Shortly after the initiation of Goals 2000, states throughout the nation began developing statewide learning standards. These standards were designed to be the baseline for curriculum and instruction in schools and districts throughout the state regardless of student income or background. Soon, along with the goals and standards, came tests designed to measure whether schools were teaching the standards effectively and, in some states, whether students would graduate or be promoted to the next grade.

In Illinois, the Illinois Learning Standards were first adopted in 1997. The standards included a list of expectations for reading, language arts (i.e., writing, listening, and speaking), mathematics, science, and social studies. Learning standards were also developed for physical education and health, art, and music. The standards were grouped by grade spans, including kindergarten through grade 2, grades 3 through 5, grades 6 through 8, and grades 9 through 12.

Shortly after Illinois adopted the Illinois Learning Standards, they mandated that schools throughout the state give the Illinois Goals Assessment Program (IGAP) test to all students at certain grade levels. The assessment reports indicated the percentage of students in individual schools and districts who achieved proficiency in each subject area. As was the case in states throughout the nation, the results of the IGAP showed serious and significant gaps in achievement between white middle class students and African American students, Latino students, students in poverty, and students with disabilities.

A few years later, the state of Illinois moved to a new test known as the Illinois Standards Achievement Test (ISAT). This test, according to state officials, more closely aligned with the Illinois Learning Standards. When the new test was given to all children in the state, the results showed lower performance for all children and a continuing achievement gap for children of color and children in poverty.

The same story can be told about many states. From Florida to Texas to California, states adopted standards and then tests to assess the standards. In every state that required testing, results showed the same patterns of achievement and underachievement.

When state officials saw that achievement was not rapidly improving and the achievement gap was not closing, they began to devise ways to hold educators accountable first for raising test scores and then for closing the achievement gap. States began developing school "report cards" designed to inform parents and communities about the quality of their schools as measured by the standardized tests. Schools' student test score data, report card grades, and other ratings that, notably, align to many of the data points in the 1969 Coleman Report were reported in the media annually.

By the time the No Child Left Behind Act, championed by President George W. Bush, was being negotiated in the halls of Congress, the notion that schools and educators should be held accountable to reach measurable goals was widely accepted as a matter of policy. Founded squarely upon the goals initiated with Goals 2000, the No Child Left Behind Act and the school reform movement continued key through lines from Goals 2000. Table 2.1 illustrates the Goals 2000 goals and through lines that serve as important aspects of our current educational system.

The No Child Left Behind Act required states to test students in reading and mathematics annually. States were required to set proficiency benchmarks and annual proficiency goals, called Adequate Yearly Progress (AYP), for each school and district. Goals for AYP were identified for each "subgroup" of students in the school or district.

Subgroups included racial/ethnic groups, socioeconomic groups, and gender groups. Under the No Child Left Behind Act, schools were required to make AYP each year until they reached 100 percent proficiency in 2014. The law also required that all teachers meet the federal definition of being Highly Qualified.

The No Child Left Behind Act was built on policies from *A Nation at Risk* and goals from Goals 2000. The No Child Left Behind Act focused on what *A Nation at Risk* called the new basics. Required testing under the act centered specifically and almost exclusively on English language arts and mathematics. The act also required testing in science in elementary, middle

Table 2.1.   Goals 2000: Educate America Act Goals and Through Lines

Area	Goals 2000 Goal	Through Lines
School Readiness	All children in America will start school ready to learn.	Early childhood program funding Kindergarten assessments
School Completion	The high school graduation rate will increase to at least 90%.	High school exit exams GED policies
Student Achievement & Citizenship	All students will leave grades 4, 8, and 12 having demonstrated competency over challenging subject matter, including English, mathematics, science, foreign languages, civics and government, economics, arts, history, and geography, and every school in America will ensure that all students learn to use their minds well so they may be prepared for responsible citizenship, further learning, and productive employment in our nation's modern economy.	Learning standards High-stakes testing Student retention in grade School report cards and grades Common Core Standards
Teacher Education & Professional Development	The nation's teaching force will have access to programs for the continued improvement of their professional skills and the opportunity to acquire the knowledge and skills needed to instruct and prepare all American students for the next century.	Continuing education requirements
Mathematics & Science	United States students will be first in the world in mathematics and science achievement.	Learning standards High-stakes testing Common Core Standards STEM education
Adult Literacy & Lifelong Learning	Every adult American will be literate and will possess the knowledge and skills necessary to compete in a global economy and exercise the rights and responsibilities of citizenship.	Learning standards College and career readiness
Safe, Disciplined, and Alcohol- and Drug-Free Schools	Every school in the United States will be free of drugs, violence, and the unauthorized presence of firearms and alcohol and will offer a disciplined environment conducive to learning.	Zero tolerance policies Police involvement in discipline

Area	Goals 2000 Goal	Through Lines
Parental Participation	Every school will promote partnerships that will increase parental involvement and participation in promoting the social, emotional, and academic growth of children.	Parent involvement policies School choice policies Charter schools

school, and high school. From Goals 2000, the No Child Left Behind Act took a focus on closing the achievement gap.

Schools and educators that failed to make AYP for the school or for a subgroup each year were subject to a variety of punishments and public scrutiny. Multiple years of failure to make AYP led to schools being designated as "failing" schools. This also triggered school choice provisions that would allow parents to request to move their children to other nonfailing schools. In addition, schools that failed to make AYP were required to use a portion of their Title I funds to provide supplemental educational services to students. These consequences were in addition to required school improvement planning and state oversight.

The No Child Left Behind Act helped to solidify and make permanent the national educational goals that began with *A Nation at Risk* and Goals 2000 and the school reform strategies that were implemented to meet them. The current generation of educators has never experienced a different approach to school improvement and accountability in their career or in their own schooling.

The No Child Left Behind Act also helped to solidify the expectation of the chronic failure of certain students in schools. Urban schools serving large populations of African American students, Latino students, and/or low-income students were rapidly identified as failing schools. For many families, the issue of failing public schools that had never been an issue for them personally became personal as their schools and children were increasingly labeled as failing.[1]

Year after year under NCLB, educators and community members were told that African American students, Latino students, and low-income students (as well as limited English proficient and disabled students) were underperforming white middle class students.

Moreover, they were told that schools that served large numbers of these students were "failing schools" and that "good schools" were being labeled as failures because of small numbers of these same groups of students. Schools with high overall achievement would fail to make AYP because their African American students, Latino students, or low-income students underperformed. In communities and the media, this was translated into "good schools" failing unfairly because of particular subgroups.

Year after year, leaders and policy makers publicly noted that African American students, Latino students, and low-income students traditionally did poorly on standardized tests. Educators and leaders commented, blogged, and debated about the cause of the achievement gap lying in student deficits or community culture or the impact of poverty. They repeatedly pointed out what they saw as the folly of expecting 100 percent proficiency.

Ten years after the advent of the No Child Left Behind Act, negative public and political opinion about the call for 100 percent proficiency, the strenuous testing requirements, and the fact that the vast majority of schools had been labeled as failing rapidly turned political leaders against the law. For several years, the US Department of Education offered waivers to states that agreed to adopt college- and career-ready standards, tie teacher and principal evaluations to test scores, and continue to test students annually.

Under the waivers, schools no longer had to offer school choice or supplemental educational services. However, they had to make the tests by which they were measured more difficult and to tie the results of those tests to individual educator performance evaluations. To obtain a waiver, each state was required to develop a plan to implement these reforms and submit it to the federal Department of Education for approval.

Impacted greatly by the politics of the time, leaders, policy makers, and community members entered a time of great debate about the federal role in education, the issue of testing, and the use of national standards. States began to call for a reduction of the federal role in education, which had only continued to grow since the passage of Goals 2000. This could have a significant impact on the achievement gap.

Many of the rights, services, and resources provided to African American students, Latino students (particularly those who were English learners), and low-income students came through federal law and federal funding. This included Title I, which provided funds to schools and districts that served a high population of students in poverty. It also included Title III, which mandated services for students with limited English proficiency and other programs such as Head Start.

These laws and the corresponding funding streams, along with Goals 2000 and NCLB, had a significant impact on states' focus on the achievement gap and the provision of services to low-income students, Latino students, and African American students. A decreased federal role in education would leave many of the decisions about services for students and the priority of closing the achievement gap to individual states with sometimes questionable records of educating all children.

Another significant part of the debate about the federal role in education focused on national learning standards. The Common Core State Standards were initially envisioned and created by representatives of the states. The Council of Chief State School Officers and the Governors Association came together around a plan to develop common educational standards that could be adopted by all states. It was argued that these standards could improve education in all the states by ensuring that students moving from state to state would be exposed to a common core of knowledge.

The Common Core State Standards could also impact the achievement gap by raising the standards in states in which proficiency standards were low (many of which included a large percentage of low-income and African American families). By designing the Common Core Standards as "college and career ready standards," the developers not only provided an operational definition for college and career ready, but they also allowed all states that adopted the Common Core State Standards to access additional federal funds through Race to the Top, a competitive federal grant program created by the Obama administration to incentivize and accelerate specific school reform policies.

After the Common Core State Standards were unveiled with much fanfare in 2010, forty-four states adopted all or most of the Common Core State Standards in English Language Arts and Mathematics as their state learning standards. Following the process established through years of school accountability from Goals 2000 to NCLB, the states then proceeded to form two consortia devoted to designing common standardized tests to assess school adherence to and student knowledge of the new standards.

The political backlash started almost immediately as conservative leaders labeled the Common Core as "ObamaCore" and began to rail against the standards as a liberal agenda and federal takeover of public education. Before long, states with conservative governors were repealing their adoption of the Common Core State Standards and issuing orders to develop their own college- and career-ready standards and standardized tests.

Along with the backlash against the Common Core Standards came a corresponding backlash against standardized testing for school accountability. Political groups and parent groups (starting with those representing primarily middle and upper middle class children) began to rebel by choosing to "opt out" of state testing on behalf of their children.

During the multiyear debate on the federal role in education and the detrimental effects of the No Child Left Behind Act, the achievement gap fell from the list of policy priorities being frequently discussed. While policy makers recognized that a gap existed that intersected with poverty and race, the policy priorities were parent choice and local control. Discussions of improving education for African American students, Latino students, and low-income students revolved around giving individual parents the ability to move out of failing public schools.

Choice proponents advocated an increase in charter schools and the provision of state-funded voucher programs to increase competition in the education arena. By ensuring competition, choice proponents posited that schools would be incentivized to improve to attract students. Schools that did not improve so they could compete would eventually close.

In practice, charter schools that were developed were funded by taking funds from public school systems. In addition, in many cases, the families with the most resources and the students with the least severe needs were the ones who obtained seats in the charter schools. Public schools in many communities were left to provide for the needs of the remaining public school students with less funding, more requirements, and less family support.

In the political environment of the decade, it took five additional years for a new federal education law to be signed. On December 10, 2015, President Barack Obama signed the Every Student Succeeds Act (ESSA) into law. This long-awaited law, yet another version of the Elementary and Secondary Education Act first adopted in 1964, repealed many aspects of the No Child Left Behind Act. However, some important policies remained, and most fundamental elements of the school accountability and reform movement continued.

Under the new law, a measure of the decision making about school accountability has returned to state legislatures. However, the law still requires annual testing in language arts and math and once-per-grade-span testing in science. It also continues to require that test scores be used as a significant factor in school accountability systems. ESSA makes each state responsible for developing a school accountability system that uses disaggregated test scores to rate each school. The accountability plans must be approved by the federal Department of Education.

The law also requires that states address the worst-performing schools (bottom 5 percent) and the worst achievement gaps in individual schools and districts. It does not, however, set a proficiency goal for all students or require states to combat the achievement gap.

In a nod to the conservative critics of the federal role in education, the ESSA places significant limits on the power of the Secretary of Education and the Department of Education to mandate or incentivize states to adopt particular standards or policies. It also loosens many of the requirements on states, allowing them to become the primary decision makers regarding overseeing education and leaving the question of whether to address the perpetuation of the achievement gap to state legislatures and departments of education.

With each step of the school accountability movement, the belief that failure is a default for low-income students, Latino students, and African American students has been reinforced. Policy makers' views of the relative importance of equity and excellence have changed during the thirty years of the school reform movement as has the federal government's involvement in promoting equity in schools. What has not changed is the presence and persistence of the achievement gap and the ideology that perpetuates it.

NOTE

1. Prior to NCLB, most families rated their own children's public schools, teachers, and leaders highly qualified even when they identified concerns with public schools as a whole.

Chapter Three

Signs and Symptoms

"The atmosphere of the home is prolonged in the school, where the students soon discover that (as in the home) in order to achieve some satisfaction they must adapt to the precepts which have been set from above. One of these precepts is not to think."

—Freire 1972

In day-to-day discussions about school reform and education policy, the unequivocal importance of the experiences of individual students in schools is often overlooked. Children learn what they experience. If educators want to change what children learn, they must attend to the experiences that children have in schools. We must recognize that although educators and leaders plan for groups of students and policy makers plan for larger society, students experience schooling as individuals.

Curriculum researchers have pointed out the difference between the intended curriculum and the implemented (or taught) curriculum. Specifically, the intended curriculum, they postulate, is the written curriculum. It is based on what is planned for educators and students. The implemented curriculum is the instruction that actually takes place in schools. The implemented curriculum differs, sometimes significantly, from the intended curriculum for a variety of reasons. Individuals' school experiences, however, differ from both the intended curriculum and the implemented curriculum.

The idea of the implemented curriculum focuses on the plans and actions of teachers in the classroom. Although this is critically important to the education students receive, it fails to encompass the complete curriculum that is taught and learned in schools. What students experience in schools on a day-to-day basis is the actual comprehensive curriculum of schools. This will be referred to as the experiential curriculum.

The experiential curriculum is made up of more than the books and resources that are used in the classroom. It is more than the learning standards that shape the school or district curriculum. It is more than the objectives and activities in the lesson plans, and it is more than the course of study that is required by the state or district.

The experiential curriculum includes the day-to-day educational and personal experiences of each individual student in the classroom. It is unique to each student. The experiential curriculum includes structures, such as the quality of the school buildings; the schedule of the day; the selection and allocation of teachers; the learning standards and objectives used by the district; the curriculum resources; the rules and procedures of the classroom, building, and district; and many other physical and nonphysical structures, parameters, rules, limits, and goals that impact the individual.

Often, even structures that are implemented for the entire district, school, or classroom have disparate impacts on the experiences of individuals. For example, the elimination of recess at the elementary level is a structural decision that impacts all students. However, this decision will affect a highly energetic second-grade boy differently than other students. One can find other examples in the day-to-day operation of schools. A student enrolled in a math class that is interrupted by a lunch period has a different experience than a student enrolled in the same class first thing in the morning or at the end of the school day.

Structures are particularly significant in schools because most of the curricular planning, instructional decisions, and administrative procedures made by educators focus on structures such as schedules, programs, procedures, and methods. Some of the most powerful structures in schools are those related to reading instruction and those related to school discipline.

The experiential curriculum also includes the many messages that students receive in and around their schools and communities about themselves, their families, their community, and education in general. Daily, students receive direct and indirect messages through the words that are shared with them; the tone that is used with them; the body language that they observe; and the things that are said to, around, or about them.

Students receive messages in other ways as well. They learn about the condition of their schools and communities through the media. They hear or see their teachers and school leaders discussing their performance, behavior, achievement, and prospects for the future. They compare what is communicated about them with what is communicated about other students in their school or students in other schools.

Students' families and community members are also directly impacted by the messages they experience. The messages can come directly through planned messages that are shared with families, or they can come indirectly through the information that is not shared with parents and families and the things that are not communicated.

Almost as important as the messages that are shared with students and their families are the messages that are shared with and among educators, policy makers, and educational leaders. Educational leaders and teacher colleagues send daily messages about their belief or disbelief in teacher and educator efficacy. They send messages about their priorities, beliefs, expectations, and aspirations. All these messages comprise part of a child's experiential curriculum.

Perhaps the most powerful aspect of the experiential curriculum is the set of attitudes and beliefs that are held by educators, leaders, policy makers, and communities. Attitudes and beliefs silently influence every decision that is made in and about schools. They create the culture in which students are immersed, indoctrinated, and assimilated. Attitudes and beliefs are the aspects of the experiential curriculum that are most readily spread. They are also the aspects of the experiential curriculum that are most resistant to intervention and change.

Attitudes and beliefs that powerfully impact children's experiential curricula can be placed into three categories. They are beliefs/attitudes about a student's identity, value (worth), and ability. In addition, educator beliefs about the purpose of schools can affect students' experiences in schools.

Structures, messages, attitudes, and beliefs shape the everyday experiences of every child in every school. What is difficult for educators and leaders to accept is the fact that the impact of this curriculum of experience outweighs positive intentions (or lack of negative intentions). It triumphs over curriculum adoptions, new learning standards and objectives, strategic initiatives, school reform strategies, and school improvement plans. The best of decisions in all these areas are easily trumped by an experiential curriculum in which students learn that educational achievement is not for people like them.

In addition, the decisions made by educators can have a disparate impact on low-income students, African American students, and Latino students.

Some students succeed regardless of the school environment. However, this is rare and should not be required for all students to succeed. African American students, Latino students, and low-income students are impacted more significantly by the quality of the experiential curriculum in schools than other students.

In 1966, James Coleman identified this phenomenon when he wrote, "The average white student's achievement seems to be less affected by the strength or weakness of his school's facilities, curriculums, and teachers than is the average minority pupil's. To put it another way, the achievement of minority pupils depends more on the schools they attend than does the achievement of majority pupils" (Coleman 1966, 22). Today, educators would say these students are school dependent.

Educators generally have a desire for children to succeed. The best teachers and administrators relish student successes, growth, and "aha" moments. They are frustrated when students struggle. However, educators, leaders, and policy makers throughout the nation have also been immersed in a curriculum of experience through which they contextualize their own work in schools. These same educators, leaders, and policy makers have the power to impact the quality of education students receive through the myriad decisions they make daily. Those decisions shape the structures, messages, attitudes, and beliefs that students experience.

Each of those decisions is made within the context of the beliefs of the larger society. Without an intentional, purposeful eye toward making strategic decisions in opposition to the status quo, educators are prone to repeatedly make decisions and recreate structures that do not serve the best interests of African American, Latino, or impoverished children.

IDENTIFYING FAILURE AS A DEFAULT

The ideology of failure as a default inspires some recurring decisions that serve to ensure the perpetuation of the achievement gap. In fact, if someone were to create a list of ways to intentionally perpetuate the achievement gap, she or he would likely identify some of the same structures, messages, and priorities that are frequently hallmarks of public schools serving large numbers of African American, Latino, and impoverished youth. See whether any of the following are familiar.

1. *Do not, under any circumstances, allow the children to become proficient readers. Ensure that they remain functionally illiterate.* It is likely unnecessary to discuss the importance of reading to combating the achievement gap. The single most effective way to limit children's academic achievement, educational attainment, and future options is to ensure that their reading comprehension level never surpasses the fifth-grade level. How do schools inadvertently do this for African American students, Latino students, and students in poverty?

- *They act as though learning to read is magic.* Because many teachers have received little or no training on teaching children to read and adults rarely recall the process through which they themselves learned how to read, teachers often assume that learning to read is supposed to happen naturally. As a result, beginning reading instruction is not structured to provide children with the foundational skills that are necessary to become readers. Educators, parents, and students themselves begin to view reading as something students either can or can't do. They neglect direct instruction of phonic and phonemic awareness.

  In the case of English learners, school programs are often structured to move English learners from their native language to English immediately or rapidly without allowing students to develop literacy in their native language. Many educators expect students to rapidly develop reading skills in their nonnative language by being immersed in an English-speaking environment. Without literacy skills in their first language, English learners often struggle to develop critical reading skills and academic vocabulary in English.

  For students who struggle with learning to read, the idea that learning to read is a mystical process that is outside their control or the control of teachers and parents promotes a sense of helplessness and inevitable failure. For parents and educators, this belief influences their expectations for students. The impact can be particularly acute for Latino students, African American students, English learners, and low-income students, for whom reading success is not viewed as guaranteed.

- *They equate difficulty learning to read with low "ability."* Because people think learning to read is automatic, they tend to believe issues with learning to read stem from learning disabilities or cognitive impairments. As a result, difficulties with learning to read or learning to comprehend high-level, complex text are treated as deficiencies within the individual child as opposed to deficiencies in instruction, curriculum, or exposure. Therefore, the response is either to try to address the individual child's deficiencies or to make peace with the idea that the child will never be a strong reader.

Children in poverty, African American children, Latino children, and English learners are disproportionately labeled with special education labels or as "slow learners." In most cases, these labels are directly tied to difficulties with learning to read.

• *They make teaching children to read the responsibility of people who are not specifically and expertly trained to teach them to read* (e.g., parents, paraprofessionals, untrained teachers). Most teachers receive precious little instruction on teaching reading in their pre-service teacher education programs. Moreover, the majority of in-service teachers gain no experience with teaching children how to read. To receive training on teaching reading, teachers generally have to pursue a master's degree in reading.

Those who do not pursue this additional training and are assigned to teach kindergarten, first, second, or third grade must often learn to teach reading by trial and error, by conducting their own online research, or by depending on other, more experienced teachers for guidance. Even with this effort and assistance, it takes years of practice to become a proficient or, better yet, a master teacher of reading. It is a shame, then, that on so many occasions well-meaning individuals with little or no training in teaching children to read are assigned this task.

Across the nation, African American, Latino, English-learner, impoverished, and disabled students who struggle with reading are the most likely students to receive some or all of their primary reading instruction from paraprofessionals, tutors, volunteers, or others who are untrained in teaching reading. Moreover, parents and family members of these students are often asked and expected to provide supplemental reading instruction. As a result, the students who are most in need of expert reading instruction rarely receive it.

This is exacerbated in situations in which parents and family members are unable to spend time teaching reading at home. The reason for this inability can vary from time constraints to lack of confidence to personal difficulties with reading. The reason does not matter. The result is that children do not receive the instruction. In addition, sometimes even the certified or licensed teacher does not possess the expertise to teach children to read. This is perhaps the most devastating situation for children.

- *They replace reading instruction with "intervention," "remediation," or other instructional replacements designed for struggling students.* Response to intervention, Reading Recovery, Title I reading instruction, and other interventions have been shown to be effective in improving children's reading skills when implemented correctly. Unfortunately, for many students, these programs are implemented in a way that removes them from core reading instruction.

Students who struggle with reading are often pulled out of their regular classroom during reading instruction to receive separate and different reading instruction in a small-group intervention setting. In these settings, they receive different instruction at a lower level individually or in a room full of other students who struggle. They miss the core curriculum, critical thinking and comprehension skills, vocabulary development, and background knowledge that are built during core literacy instruction. In addition, they quickly become unable to interact and discuss the same topics as students who are performing at grade level in the classroom.

When this kind of intervention begins early in elementary school, it has an exponential impact on students' academic and social growth. By fourth grade, these students can be identified by educators, parents, peers, and most importantly themselves as academic and social outliers. Anyone who has worked in schools knows what this means for student development and behavior.

- *They neglect or delay teaching comprehension and critical thinking skills.* A variation of this is they act as though thinking and comprehension are skills the students either have or don't have and not things that are taught. In 2000, the National Reading Panel identified the five component skills for reading instruction. They were phonemic awareness, phonics, fluency, vocabulary, and comprehension (National Reading Panel 2000).

Unfortunately, schools that serve African American, Latino, English-learner, and impoverished students as well as educators who serve students who struggle with reading sometimes treat these skills as linear. In other words, instead of addressing all these skills simultaneously, they treat them as stairsteps, with phonemic awareness being taught before phonics, phonics being taught before fluency, fluency being taught before vocabulary, and vocabulary being taught before comprehension. For English learners, educators may believe they need to develop English-language skills prior to teaching vocabulary and comprehension skills. By delaying exposure to and instruction in vocabulary and comprehension, educators inadvertently allow students to fall further and further behind their peers.

2. *Place the children in classrooms with teachers who lack the skill, knowledge, talent, dedication, or desire to ensure their success. For best results, ensure that the children have at least two such teachers in a row.* Schools have a history of selecting and retaining teachers for students because they are nice, they fit in, they have seniority, they work hard, they are cheap, they love children, or they are "warm bodies" who are available to do the job. This means the students who are most dependent on being taught by outstandingly talented, dedicated, highly skilled teachers are rarely assigned to the kind of educator they need. How do schools inadvertently contribute to this?

   • *They fail to recognize the importance of talent when they recruit and select teachers and leaders. They act as though training alone can make someone a teacher or leader.* Like most other professions, teaching and school leadership require an individual to possess specific talents. Although skills can be taught, talents such as empathy; building rapport; the ability to discern student needs, strengths, and misconceptions; and the ability to create environments of safety and wonder for children can be enhanced only where they already exist.

   The nature of teacher education and the teacher selection process in most schools and districts is such that knowledge, skills, and experience are taken into consideration while talent is not.

- *They assign students to classes or schedules without regard for the needs of the students or the varying strengths and weaknesses of the teachers.* It is an often-unspoken reality that some teachers are generally more effective than others and some are more successful with certain types of students than others. Educators and administrators know that this is the case as do parents who have had multiple children go through the school system.

  In some cases, this distinction is between highly effective teachers with different styles and different classroom environments. In other cases, the distinction is between teachers who are effective at making connections with students, structuring positive environments, and improving student learning and teachers who are missing the talent and/or skills to be effective. Either way, educators and leaders tend to ignore the distinctions except in cases where parents refuse to go along with the fiction and request that their children be placed with (or not placed with) a specific educator.

  The result for low-income students, African American students, and Latino students, whose parents are less likely to possess the capital to request and receive special placement, is an increased likelihood that they will be in nonpreferred classrooms or in classrooms that were not specifically chosen to meet their needs.

- *They neglect professional development and allow teacher and leader skills to stagnate at the novice level.* It is well known in education circles that the professional development of preservice teachers is insufficient to prepare teachers for the intensity of the requirements and expectations of the teaching profession. Most teachers enter the profession with a four-year degree of which only three semesters are devoted to teaching strategies and methods.

  Depending on the state in which teacher education takes place, preservice teachers may be required to take one course on special education, one course on child development or educational psychology, one introduction to teaching course, and one course each on methods for teaching reading, mathematics, science, and social studies. Upon completion of their methods courses, preservice teachers participate in a four- to eight-month internship known as student teaching.

  In many states, preservice teachers are not required to receive training in serving English learners or meeting the needs of students with disabilities. In addition, most teacher preparation programs require little or no coursework or practicum experiences on teaching in racially, ethnically, and socioeconomically diverse school settings.

Teachers develop proficiency and grow into master teachers while on the job. However, the process of professional growth does not happen automatically. Without ongoing attention to professional development and growth, teachers can continue to operate at a novice teacher level even when they are veteran teachers.

- *They label teachers as "good" or "bad" based on numerous measures other than students' experiences and learning in the classroom.* Teaching is a noble profession that is filled primarily with individuals who love children and have good intentions. Unfortunately, good intentions do not necessarily equate to high levels of talent, strong skills, or effectiveness.

Educators and leaders tend to label themselves and their colleagues as good teachers based on their intentions, love for children, and work ethic. This can be detrimental to professional growth when educators stop working to improve or when they decide that they do not need to change their practices because they are already good teachers.

In addition, when educators and leaders see themselves as good or bad, it is very difficult for them to closely examine their practices to improve student outcomes. The thought seems to be that if someone is a good teacher and the student doesn't learn, the problem must reside within the student. If someone is a bad teacher and the student doesn't learn, the teacher will not be able to improve student outcomes anyway because he or she is a bad teacher.

One common refrain when teachers are trained in a new or different method of teaching is the statement that the new method is "just good teaching." This mind-set discourages teachers from trying new things because they feel that since they are good teachers they are already implementing the new method or technique.

All these ways of thinking are detrimental to African American, Latino, and impoverished youth because many of the methods teachers learn in preservice teacher education have not been found to be effective with these groups of students. Teachers must continually gain new skills and try new best practices to meet the needs of all students.

- *They devote time to attempting to change long-standing teacher and leader biases and prejudices by invoking sympathy.* In the attempt to address the biases and prejudices that are common among all human beings, educational leaders and student advocates often institute programs aimed at getting teachers to understand the plight of students in poverty and/or the cultural differences between them and the students they teach.

These programs and activities are particularly important in settings in which the student population has shifted to include more students in poverty or more students from a different racial or ethnic group than most of the teachers. They can assist teachers who want to understand the different perspectives and lived experiences of their students and families. However, without targeted, specific planning for how these perspectives will be used to improve students' school experiences, these programs and activities do not positively impact student experiences or student achievement.

More importantly, for teachers and leaders with strongly held biases and those without a willingness to value other perspectives, these activities often serve to reinforce stereotypes, lower expectations, and produce feelings of pity or disdain. This, in turn, works against student learning and achievement.

3. *Eliminate everything that does not directly address test scores and replace it with test prep and other activities designed specifically for raising test scores.* The testing requirements and consequences of the No Child Left Behind Act led not only to a narrowing of the planned curriculum to only tested subjects but also to the abandonment of recess and other developmentally appropriate and social, emotionally necessary but untested subjects. How do schools fall into this trap?

- *They eliminate recess and physical education to gain additional "instructional time."* By eliminating daily recess and daily physical education, schools believe they can recoup up to sixty minutes of "instructional time." Unfortunately, when schools take this approach, they end up with a net loss of instructional effectiveness. This is particularly the case for male students.

Students who do not have safe, unstructured, or choice-based time during the instructional day are more likely to demonstrate attention deficits, high levels of stress, and behavioral issues. This impacts instructional effectiveness.

In addition, unstructured and choice-based playtime provides opportunities for students to develop and use social, executive-functioning, and decision-making skills that are not developed in settings in which the use of time, rules, and procedures are highly structured and imposed instead of negotiated among peers. Recess and physical education are not simply for letting "kids be kids." They provide opportunities for students to use and strengthen skills that are also important for life beyond school.

Low-income students, Latino students, and African American students in urban or low-achieving schools are the most likely students to be deprived of physical education and recess.

- *They treat instruction in areas such as art, music, speech, and drama like "extras" or privileges.* Elements of the curriculum that focus on creativity and other untestable skills are often the first to go when schools attempt to make funding cuts or rapidly raise student test scores. Schools sometimes eliminate instruction in these areas to save money and time. This typically starts with reductions to the amount of time spent on these subjects.

  Exposure to these elements of a liberal arts education is an expectation in middle class environments, colleges, and universities and in white-collar careers. Deprived of instruction in and exposure to fine and performing arts, speech, and leadership, students fall further behind their middle class and wealthy peers.

- *They eliminate (usually through neglect) instruction in areas necessary for a high level of future success, such as writing, social studies/history, leadership, and civics and lab science.* The No Child Left Behind Act and its successor, the Every Student Succeeds Act, mandated statewide testing and accountability requirements in reading, math, and science. In the pursuit of Adequate Yearly Progress (AYP), many schools serving diverse populations have abandoned instruction in curricular areas that are not tested for measuring accountability.

  At the start of NCLB, the State of Illinois implemented tests in reading, math, writing, science, and social studies. Over time, the

State Board of Education eliminated the social studies test. A few years later, they eliminated the writing test. Within two years of the elimination of these tests, schools throughout the state (particularly the low-achieving ones) had reduced or eliminated direct instruction in social studies and writing.

In some schools, this happened when leaders made formal curricular decisions. In far more schools, this happened through neglect as teachers and leaders placed less and less emphasis on these subjects and more and more on reading and math.

This narrowing of the curriculum was particularly acute in low-achieving schools and schools with limited resources. High-achieving schools and schools serving students in wealthy communities continued to teach a complete curriculum to provide their students with skills and experiences necessary for success. African American students, Latino students, and students in poverty suffer from the disadvantage of a narrow, incomplete curriculum.

- *They abandon pedagogy in favor of "foolproof" drills, workbooks, and software applications.* Another response to high-stakes testing has been a loss of trust in and dependence on teachers to plan and implement effective instruction. There has, for some school districts, been a corresponding withdrawal of investment in teacher and leader education.

There is an active market for test prep curricula and instructional "solutions" that promise to raise student performance on high-stakes tests. These products are promoted as being data-based, teacher-friendly, standards-aligned, and sometimes interactive. These terms are used to persuade leaders that the use of the test prep and other instructional solutions will provide improved outcomes for any children in any setting with any teachers.

When schools adopt these programs, they typically focus all professional development and training on implementing the program. This often comes at the detriment of other professional development programs as well as other subject areas. In addition, schools that adopt these programs tend to remove the focus from teacher pedagogy and planning based on the needs of the students and focus on implementing a standardized, foolproof program.

4. *Treat children with suspicion, distrust, and disdain. Imagine the worst outcomes for them (e.g., prison, poverty, delinquency) and treat them as though those negative outcomes have already occurred.* When educators distrust the children they serve or believe they are doomed to delinquency, they respond more harshly to perceived misbehavior. Schools in districts that serve larger numbers of African American, Latino, and low-income students and schools in urban or "inner-city" settings tend to implement more restrictive disciplinary codes, policies, and disciplinary actions. This results in high rates of suspensions, expulsions, and other removals from instruction. What do schools do to contribute to this?

- *They make the consequences of mistakes and misbehavior so severe that it is impossible for students to recover.* Unrecoverable consequences include restrictive discipline, such as suspension and expulsion. However, they also include actions that do not rise to the level of traditional school discipline. Such actions include long-term social isolation, shaming in front of peers, use of aggression to hurt or intimidate children, and denial or termination of relationships within the school. Each of these actions jeopardizes or destroys the positive relationships that are necessary for students to fully engage in learning.

  For African American children, in particular, the loss of relationship with teachers and other adults at school is devastating. African American community members tend to view education as a transaction that takes place primarily between the student and the teacher (Hill 2011). If the student-teacher relationship is damaged or nonexistent, learning and growth will also be hindered. African American children, Latino children, and low-income children are disproportionately disciplined in ways that destroy relationships or that make recovery unlikely.

- *They adopt and adhere to "zero tolerance" policies.* Zero tolerance policies came into favor beginning with the federal crime bills passed in the early 1990s that intensified the response to crime. The crime bill imposed minimum sentences for drug crimes and violence. Many states followed suit with intensified responses to misbehavior and crime in schools. This process of criminalizing misbehavior in schools accelerated in 2000 after the massacre at Columbine High School.

Zero tolerance policies require school officials to institute severe disciplinary actions for specific infractions regardless of the circumstances of the misbehavior. In some cases, policy or practice requires law enforcement involvement in the process as well. Groups such as the Children's Defense Fund have labeled the criminalization of school misbehavior and the application of zero tolerance policies and law enforcement methods to school discipline issues as the "school-to-prison pipeline."[1]

Low-income children, African American children, and Latino children, especially males, make up a disproportionate part of the school-to-prison pipeline. More schools serving predominately African American and Latino students and more schools in urban areas with large numbers of low-income students utilize these tactics.

- *They routinely remove students from instruction for behaviors.* The most common consequence given to students for disruptive, distracted, or disrespectful behavior is removal from instruction. This comes in the form of time-out seclusion, in-school suspension, out-of-school suspension, office referrals, "sitting out," and in-school detention. Each removal has a negative impact on student learning.

  The impact of removal from instruction is compounded when students are routinely given this consequence. Students for whom this is the case, sometimes referred to as "frequent flyers," are unable to experience continuity of curriculum and instruction or full integration into the classroom environment. African American students, Latino students, and students in poverty are disproportionately disciplined in ways that remove them from instruction.

- *They select disciplinary consequences to hurt or get back at students.* One of the most common and detrimental mistakes educators make in establishing school and classroom discipline programs is striving to punish students for misbehavior. Instead of selecting consequences that are logical in nature and aimed at ending the behavior, educators sometimes select consequences to elicit an emotional response from the student. The goal for these educators is to ensure that the student feels punished.

When confronted by punishments or consequences that are designed to cause pain, students rebel, fight back, or withdraw. The reaction of a student depends on his or her personality, culture, and prior experiences. For many African American children, fighting back or resisting real or perceived oppression is a cultural value (Hill 2011). As a result, it is not uncommon for African American children to exhibit this tendency.

For all students, the realization that their teacher is willing and able to hurt them negatively impacts the relationship between the teacher and student. Because many adults in school do not understand the responses of African American students, Latino students, and low-income students to correction and redirection, they are more likely to attempt to garner an emotional response from their use of discipline. This fact, along with the fact that these groups of students, particularly males, receive more and harsher punishments in general, adds to the achievement gap.

5. *Allow students to develop or assist them in developing high aspirations, but be careful to ensure that they have neither the knowledge of what it takes to achieve those goals nor the skills to do what it takes to succeed.* As the push toward college and career readiness has progressed, many schools, communities, and families have embraced the aspiration for all or most children to go to four-year colleges or universities. The difficulty for many students is that while they have been exposed to the idea of attending college, they have been falsely convinced that going to college is as simple as having the aspiration and making the decision to attend. When the realities of the difficulties and inequities of attending and succeeding in postsecondary education become evident, students can quickly become disillusioned. What do schools do to exacerbate this problem?

- *They treat rites of passage such as high school and middle school graduation like terminal events.* At one high school graduation, the seniors' graduation song was titled "The Struggle Is Over." A parent at a middle school graduation took pictures and reflected that "this may be the only graduation my child gets to see." A high school curriculum committee determined that students would not have to write a research paper or essays in the regular-level classes because such activities were necessary only for college-bound students who should be in honors classes.

Educators, leaders, and community members sometimes send the message that the completion of high school or middle school is the end goal for schools and students. As a result, both students and educators can make shortsighted decisions that serve to limit students' options past middle school and high school. In addition, this way of thinking often results in graduates feeling lost and disillusioned because they have never prepared for life beyond graduation and they do not have any strategies in place to meet educational, career, or life goals.

- *They provide classes labeled as college preparatory without preparing students for the expectations of college coursework.* Prior to the push toward college and career readiness, students who were considered to be college bound were placed in honors-level courses because those courses were seen as college preparatory. Since the focus shifted to college and career readiness, many high schools have designated their regular- or middle-track classes as "college prep" courses. However, in many cases, the courses are no different than they were prior to being designated as college prep. As a result, students in the college prep track do not receive the level of instruction and expectations that have traditionally been expected for students entering college.

Another example of this is when schools offer Advanced Placement (AP) classes, International Baccalaureate (IB) classes, and college preparatory programs such as AVID, but fail to provide students with the full resources and exposure that are expected as part of the program. This includes offering AP and IB science courses without lab requirements; offering AP and IB language arts courses without significant writing expectations; offering AP and IB history and social science courses without high expectations for reading, research, and writing; or hosting an AVID program without having authentic discussions about the academic, financial, social, and cultural challenges of college admission and completion.

Latino students, African American students, and low-income students continue to attend schools with fewer honors, AP, and IB offerings in general. When schools serving these students do offer these programs, they are less likely to provide the full resources, exposure, and expectations provided to middle and upper class white students in the same programs. In high-income schools that offer the full scope of AP, IB, and honors programs, low-income students, Latino students, and African American students are typically underrepresented in those programs.

- *They neglect the development of leadership, communication, problem-solving, and self-advocacy skills.* The college environment creates a culture shock for many students. This is particularly the case for students who are first-generation college students and for students who are attending schools in which they are an underrepresented minority. To get into and successfully complete college, students must possess the skills necessary to effectively advocate for themselves, navigate new environments, negotiate to ensure that their needs are met, and persevere through new challenges.

All these skills are in addition to the academic skills necessary to complete the college coursework. In addition, particularly for low-income students and first-generation college students, financial understanding and financial management skills are critically important to ensure that students are able to complete their college education.

In schools that serve large numbers of low-income students, not only are these skills not directly taught as a part of the planned curriculum, but they are undermined as a part of the experiential curriculum. Schools that promote learning by rote, excessive test prep; high levels of tracking; and other symptoms of failure as a default deter students from actively advocating for their needs, communicating their desires effectively, and negotiating to get their needs met. In addition, these schools typically serve students whose families lack the social capital to use these skills to obtain advantages within the school community. As a result, the students neither experience using these skills firsthand nor witness these skills being used by those who are closest to them.

6. *If a child has the inclination to focus and work hard, focus her or his time, energy, and talent on things that will take up a great deal of time but provide little or no long-term educational benefit.* Educators and leaders are often inspired by students who demonstrate particular talent, focus, desire, and resilience. These students have the potential to

overcome their circumstances and achieve a level of success that is far beyond the ordinary. However, schools often fail these students by neglecting to guide them through the real-world steps and give them the requisite skills to meet their goals. How do educators and leaders do this?

- *They place students who struggle on a parallel track to the planned curriculum. They formally or informally track students based on their perceived or predicted ability.* When students are removed from the general curriculum for any reason, they lose access to the planned curriculum. In the attempt to assist students who struggle, schools have implemented programs and courses that run parallel to the curriculum. Once a student is removed to the parallel track, he or she is never on track to merge with the learning standards.

This can take the form of traditional school-wide tracking practices that place students in a remedial, regular, advanced, or honors track. It can also take the form of other programs that are initially designed to help students who struggle with particular skills. Any program, no matter how well-intentioned, that causes students to become trapped in a parallel curriculum that does not allow for movement has the impact of limiting student growth and achievement.

Because of the history of low achievement of African American, Latino, and low-income students, the students fill the remedial tracks, classes, and programs.

- *They minimize the importance of academic skills and achievement for students who have nonacademic gifts and talents (e.g., music, sports).* For some students, their physical, artistic, or other gifts are seen as their ticket to college and/or lifetime success. Talented football, basketball, soccer, and track athletes along with gifted musicians, vocalists, actors, dancers, artists, and others with special talents are recruited by many colleges and universities. However, in the absence of careful planning and balanced priorities, these students can be placed in situations in which they cannot take advantage of the educational opportunities offered to them or they do not have the skills to complete the education programs they start.

This often happens when schools routinely remove students from instruction to perform or play, when educators and leaders waive or relax academic standards for students, or when they allow students and families to belief that their talents alone will guarantee their success regardless of their academic skills.

7. *Treat failure as the default condition for the child, his family, his community, and the other children he perceives to be like him. Reassure him and those around him that any level of achievement by him is acceptable because it is better than predicted.* Schools that serve African American students, low-income students, and Latino students send the message that failure and underachievement are routine and expected in myriad ways. These messages are clear to students and to their families and serve to teach students that high achievement is not expected from children like them. How do schools send the message that failure is a default?

- *They opt not to share students' assessment results with their families, or they do so in a way that obscures negative information.* Under the No Child Left Behind Act and the subsequent Every Student Succeeds Act, schools are required to assess students annually. Most schools assess student performance multiple times each year and use the results of those assessments to make numerous decisions for and about students. However, schools vary in the degree to which they share assessment information with families.

  Particularly in schools in which student achievement as measured by standardized tests is low, educators often decide not to share test score information that shows that a student is not performing at the desired level. They may do this by simply declining to provide the information to families, by burying the information in a flurry of other papers or pieces of information, by neglecting to provide the information in the family's native language, by downplaying the importance or meaning of the assessments, or by presenting the information in a way that hides the comparison of the student's score to the expectation.

- *They use past performance to set expectations for acceptable future performance.* One frequent, and troubling, strategy used in some data analytics models for education is using the past performance of a student or group of students to predict the future performance for individual students and to determine the acceptable amount of growth for the student. This approach has become more prevalent as states, districts, and individual schools have shifted the accountability focus to student growth in test scores and used these growth measures as a part of "value-added" models for teacher and program evaluation.

In these models, statisticians review the prior test score achievement and growth for a group of students, such as Latino students. They use this information to calculate the typical growth for a student in this group. Then, they use that typical growth as the growth goal for the next year. If a student meets that growth expectation, he or she is considered to have met the expectation. If a student surpasses that growth expectation, his or her teacher is credited for "value added."

The problem with this approach is that students from groups that have traditionally been on the losing side of the achievement gap have their growth goals set based on past underachievement. As a result, continued underachievement is celebrated as meeting growth goals. This skewed view of the level at which students should be able to perform impacts both the students and the educators who come to embrace the low expectations as appropriate.

• *They use their demographics as an excuse or justification for student outcomes.* One of the negative impacts of the No Child Left Behind assessment data and reporting has been the pressure placed on leaders and educators to explain the reason for low achievement scores for subgroups of students. The desire to maintain the image of being a good school has led many leaders to use the acceptance of failure as a default as a way to justify student outcomes on standardized tests and to excuse schools and districts from the responsibility of improving outcomes for low-income, Latino, African American, and other groups of students.

The frequent refrain, when school and district leaders attempt to explain the low achievement of student subgroups is "We are a good school. We did not make AYP because of our _____ subgroup." This is typically followed by an explanation that those subgroups have traditionally done poorly on standardized tests, that the group represents only a small number of students in the school or district, that schools cannot overcome the impact of poverty, or some other explanation that is grounded in the achievement gap ideology.

The result of this reaction to low achievement for some students is that a clear message is sent to students, communities, educators, and leaders that low achievement for some students is par for the course. Like many of the other actions and decisions on this list, the tendency of leaders to justify or excuse low achievement for African American, Latino, and low-income students helps to promote a lack of urgency and efficacy on the part of school educators and leaders.

- *They make curriculum selections and decisions based on the perceived low abilities of their students.* Choice of curriculum is one of the key decisions made by educators that impacts student achievement. When failure is a default, educators and leaders view curriculum resources through the lens of their beliefs about what their students can be expected to achieve. As a result, educators and leaders serving low-income, Latino, and African American students tend to select resources that are at a lower level than what is expected for middle class students. Moreover, in whatever curriculum or program they are using, educators and leaders make instructional decisions that are strongly influenced by their view of their students' abilities.

- *They determine which children, schools, and communities "count" based on test scores and perceived potential.* One of the worst responses to the requirements of the No Child Left Behind Act has been the practice of designating students as those who "count" and those who do not "count" for school accountability. Under NCLB, a student enrolled in a school for less than a certain amount of time (approximately one school year in most states) was required to take the state standardized test, but the results of that test would not be included in the results for the school or district. This was rapidly translated into each student being categorized as either counting or not counting.

This determination impacted the services that were available to students because schools focused their instructional interventions, after-school programs, and other services on the students who counted. Many schools took it a step further by dividing the students who counted into groups based on how close they were to meeting the standards on the state standardized test. Students who were within a few points of passing the tests (known as "bubble kids") were given extra instruction while students who were significantly behind were not. In this way, educators and leaders tried to focus their resources to get the best possible improvement in test scores for the available resources.

The result of focusing resources on students that educators identify as counting is that other students fall further and further behind and that students and their families learn that their test scores are what matter to educators and leaders.

Table 3.1 provides a checklist of these signs and symptoms that demonstrate the presence and impact of failure as a default in a school or district. The list is not exhaustive; it simply includes some of the most prevalent structures, messages, and beliefs that impact the experiential curriculum children receive in schools. If these signs and symptoms exist in a school, it is time for educators and leaders to confront failure as a default.

EXPERIENTIAL CURRICULUM AUDITS

On a visit to Ms. Slater's first-grade classroom, I met Markus. When I entered the classroom, the class was engaged in learning centers. While Ms. Slater conducted a guided reading group at the kidney table in the back of the room, the other students worked on a variety of activities. As I walked around the classroom, I noticed Markus, a six-year-old African American boy, staring at the worksheet in front of him with tears in his eyes. When he just sat there looking frustrated and defeated for over a minute, I made my way to his desk.

When I addressed him, he let the tears fall as he said, "I can't do it. It's too hard." The worksheet in front of Markus included several addition equations with sums to twenty. I wiped Markus's tears and summoned up my most convincing "Oh, yes, you can! Let's try it!" I showed Markus the number line on his desk. Together, we used the number line to count on ($11 + 3 = 14$). Then, I asked Markus to show me where to start for the next equation ($9 + 6 = 15$). He went on to lead me through questions 2 and 3, and then I cheered him as he completed numbers 4 and 5 on his own.

My interaction with Markus made me both curious and concerned about his plight. As a first-grader, he had already developed a sense that he could

Table 3.1.   Symptoms of Failure as a Default

Schools in which failure is a default . . .	Does your school or district . . .
Do not allow students to become proficient readers.	<ul><li>Treat learning to read like magic.</li><li>Equate difficulty with learning to read with low ability.</li><li>Make teaching reading the responsibility of people who are not trained.</li><li>Replace reading instruction with intervention or remediation.</li><li>Neglect or delay teaching reading comprehension and critical thinking.</li></ul>
Place students with teachers who cannot or will not ensure their success.	<ul><li>Ignore talent in teacher recruitment and selection.</li><li>Neglect professional development and allow skills to stagnate.</li><li>Label teachers as good or bad without regard for student learning.</li><li>Invoke sympathy to change long-standing biases.</li></ul>
Eliminate anything that does not raise test scores and replace it with test prep.	<ul><li>Take away recess and physical education.</li><li>Treat such areas as art, music, and speech as extras.</li><li>Eliminate untested subject areas.</li><li>Replace pedagogy with drills, software, and test prep.</li></ul>
Treat some students with suspicion and distrust.	<ul><li>Make consequences too severe to allow recovery.</li><li>Adopt zero tolerance policies.</li><li>Remove students from instruction for behavior.</li><li>Choose consequences to hurt students.</li></ul>
Allow students to develop high aspirations without the skills to achieve.	<ul><li>Treat graduations as terminal events.</li><li>Offer college prep courses that fail to prepare students for college coursework.</li><li>Neglect the development of self-advocacy and other key skills.</li></ul>
Focus students' time on things that provide little or no long-term benefit.	<ul><li>Place students on a parallel track to the core curriculum.</li><li>Minimize the importance of academic achievement in favor of nonacademic talents.</li></ul>
Treat failure as the default condition for the child, his family, and his community.	<ul><li>Decide not to share student assessment results with families.</li><li>Use past performance to set expectations for the future.</li><li>Use demographics as an excuse for student outcomes.</li><li>Make curricular selections based on perceived low student ability.</li><li>Designate students as those who "count" and those who do not count.</li></ul>

not do his schoolwork. His tears at not knowing how to do what was asked of him spoke volumes about his experiences in school.

In addition to reviewing practices to identify failure as a default, educators and leaders must develop the ability to analyze how those practices impact children. Many school and district leaders find themselves removed from schools, classrooms, and individual students. They access assessment data, school improvement plans, and other information to make meaningful decisions on behalf of their students. However, the only real way to gain an understanding of the experiences of students in schools is to meet and observe the students.

One of the most powerful ways to identify the structures, messages, and attitudes that perpetuate the achievement gap in a school or district is by paying focused attention to the daily experiences of the children who are on the losing side of the educational balance. A key method of doing this is conducting an experiential curriculum audit. This is necessary to gain access to the experiential curriculum without the blinders of the planned curriculum, the numerous initiatives that take place in the school, or the positive intentions of educators.

In an experiential curriculum audit, a leader identifies one or more individual students whose achievement or growth is below the standard. The leader then conducts an educational case study of that student's experiences to identify the experiences that contribute to underachievement as well as opportunities for improvement.

The process of conducting an experiential audit begins with identifying target students who struggle and gathering key information about the students' experiences in school. Using the information gathered about individual students, school leaders can draw conclusions through interpolation and extrapolation and plan for school improvement.

The target student should be a child from a group of students who underperform. It is helpful if the student also has a history of two or more years within the district. This is important because it allows the leader to track the student's experiences and progress through his or her time in the system.

The next step is to review the student's academic history, achievement data, and schedule history. What do the records show about the student's skills? What are the student's relative areas of strength and weakness? How have the student's skills progressed over time? Have there been periods of growth or stagnation for the student? Which school(s) has the student attended? Who has taught the student? The goal at this stage is to learn as much about the student as possible from the traditional information available to school and district leaders.

At this point, the leader conducting the audit should avoid reviewing disciplinary data and information about the student's family background. Such information can cloud one's view of the experiences of the student by causing the observer to draw premature conclusions about the reasons for the student's underachievement.

After reviewing the available data about the student, the next step is to visit the student to observe the experiential curriculum in which he or she is immersed. This is the core of the experiential curriculum audit. Visit the student in the classroom setting on different days, at different times, and during different subjects. It is most helpful if both teachers and students are accustomed to the auditor visiting the school and classroom. The auditor's goal is to observe the interactions as they occur naturally and not to have either the teacher or the students put on a show or behave in a way that is out of the ordinary.

A classroom visit can be as short as five or ten minutes at a time. Upon entering the classroom setting, the auditor should consider her or his initial observations and reactions and then quickly hone in on the perspective of the target student. It is key that the auditor's focus is not on the teacher's actions or performance and that the observations are not evaluative in nature for the teacher or the student. In addition, the auditor should not focus on trying to determine why the student is underachieving.

This approach all too often leads to the assignment or assumption of blame, which is counterproductive to the improvement process. The focus and goal are to see the classroom from the target student's point of view, to gauge the curriculum the individual student is experiencing, and to identify and eliminate elements of failure as a default that help perpetuate the achievement gap for that student and for other students like him or her.

The target student does not need to know that she or he is the focus of the observation. It is best to make the idea that someone is observing the child's learning a routine reality. The target student should feel no different than any other student in the class. This can typically be achieved by observing and interacting with other students as well.

During the observations, the auditor should ask herself or himself questions regarding the structures, messages, attitudes, and beliefs that make up the child's experiential curriculum. Under structures, the auditor would consider such things as the physical environment of the classroom, where the child is seated, the child's schedule, the classroom management system, and the use of time.

Regarding messages, thought should be given to the verbal and nonverbal messages in the classroom, such as announcements or statements made to the whole class, statements made to one student or group of students that can be overheard by others, body language between the target student and the teacher and between the target student and other students, and educator word choice and tone.

Attitudes and beliefs should also be considered. Although it is often impossible to identify educators' attitudes and beliefs without talking with them directly, it is important to remember that the auditor's goal is not to determine what educators think or believe. Instead, it is to determine how the student may experience and interpret educator and leader attitudes and beliefs.

Based on what we know about educational psychology and human development, it makes sense that children of all ages are strongly influenced by their experiences, that they internalize many of the messages they receive from adults, and that they interpret and are impacted by their interpretations of the attitudes and beliefs of the adults around them. Observations of the experiential curriculum can reveal volumes about the experiences students have in schools that communicate failure as a default.

For example, on a visit to a first-grade classroom, an auditor observed as a target student participated in a small-group math lesson. The teacher had established the routine that when a student answered a question correctly, he or she got to ring a bell that was on the table. On this day, the target student raised his hand to answer a question. The teacher called on him, but the student answered the question incorrectly. The teacher asked the student to think about it and prompted him to modify his answer.

The student worked through it and finally came up with the correct answer, much to his relief. The teacher said, "That is correct" and moved on to the next question. The target student paused for a moment before saying, "Can I ring the bell?" The teacher replied, "No. You don't get to ring the bell because you didn't answer the question perfectly the first time."

Another target student was in fourth grade when an auditor came to observe her during the reading block. The teacher asked the class to turn to page 162 in their reading books. The target student put her book on her desk and then went to get a tissue. She stood by the garbage can blowing and wiping her nose for just over a minute before slowing walking back to her seat.

When she got there, the target student got out her pencil box and started looking for the pencil with just the right tip. She took it out and then began examining the other pencils in the box. With prompting from an adult, she finally opened her book to page 162 to catch up with the discussion that was taking place just as another teacher arrived at the classroom door to take her to receive her thirty minutes of reading intervention for the day.

In another classroom with a target student, the auditor observed as the student participated in a whole-group math lesson. The teacher modeled solving the first math problem. She then guided the students through the second math problem before stating aloud, "I'm not going to give you all the next one because it is really difficult."

In each of these cases, the auditor must analyze the structures, messages, attitudes, and beliefs that impact the target students. In all cases, the educators' intentions appeared to be positive. However, for the purpose of auditing the experiential curriculum, intentions do not matter.

In the first case, when the teacher refused to allow the student to ring the bell, one of the messages the student received was that only perfect answers obtained without struggle, assistance, or prompting were valued. From this message, the student may have concluded (as evidenced by decreased risk taking during subsequent lessons) that it was not worth it to try to answer a question unless she or he was sure her or his answer would be correct. Further, the student may have concluded that effort and perseverance are not valued. These unplanned lessons were taught through experience and not through the written curriculum.

In the second case, instruction progressed as planned, but the student missed the core reading instruction as she participated in activities aside from the lesson and, then, as she was removed to receive reading intervention. Not only did the student not learn what was being taught during the reading block, but she also may have learned how easily she could avoid participating in reading instruction.

In the final example, the target student (and all the other students) was impacted by the teacher's belief that the math problem in the grade-level math book was too difficult. First, this belief caused the student not to be exposed to the more challenging problems. Since the problem was part of the grade-level math curriculum, the teacher was unknowingly limiting the student's progress in math by avoiding challenging work. Second, because the teacher shared the belief that the problem was difficult, the student may have interpreted the teacher's belief as a lack of confidence in the student's ability, as an indication that grade-level work is too difficult for him or students like him or as a statement that math in general is hard.

It is only by strategically observing the experiences students have in schools that educators and leaders can begin to understand the full impact of their decisions on students. As they develop that understanding, educators and leaders can begin to identify and change the structures, messages, attitudes, and beliefs that perpetuate the achievement gap and communicate that failure is a default for low-income students, African American students, and Latino students.

NOTE

1. The Children's Defense Fund has devoted its efforts to ending the school-to-prison pipeline (www.childrensdefensefund.org).

Chapter Four

Write the Vision

"In these days, it is doubtful that any child may reasonably be expected to succeed in life if he is denied the opportunity of an education. Such an opportunity, where the state has undertaken to provide it, is a right which must be made available to all on equal terms."

—*Brown v. Board of Education* 1954

The lack of a vision of success for all children is a key driver of failure as a default. Successive generations of educators, families, and leaders operate in schools without any conception of schools designed for the success of all children. Failure as a default is so ingrained in our consciousness that it is difficult to think about schools differently.

Can there be a better way? Is America as a nation finally ready to design schools for success for every child? What might a school designed to prepare all children for current and future success look like?

To create schools in which all children are prepared to succeed, educators, leaders, and policy makers must be ready to combat a core idea that has shaped how schooling is provided in the United States. They must combat the widespread idea that some groups of students deserve better educational opportunities and outcomes than others based on the merits of their identity, the circumstances of their birth, or the work or resources of their parents, communities, and families.[1] The belief that inequality is acceptable because some families, parents, and communities care more, contribute more, or deserve more stands in opposition to ending failure as a default.

Although the concept of meritocracy is an American cultural value, its application to education stands in stark contrast to the American ideal of equality. In addition, the application of meritocracy to the quality of education provided to children jeopardizes the economic, cultural, and political standing and future of the United States. The pre-K through twelfth-grade population of the United States is now over 50 percent low income and over 50 percent minority (National Center for Education Statistics 2016). The number and percentage of low-income students and minority students are projected to continue to rise through the next decade.

It is impossible to sustain the standards of education and economic and civic engagement that have made the United States a great political and economic superpower while proceeding to provide a high-quality liberal arts and sciences education to smaller and smaller portions of the population. By accepting the idea that the only children who should receive the highest quality of education are those whose parents and communities have and expend the time, money, social standing, knowledge, and political power to acquire better resources for their children, society resigns itself to the inevitable result of inaction—widespread and intransigent inequality and underachievement.

For many middle and upper class families, the provision of education is focused on conferring upon the next generation the same or better status or privileges as are enjoyed by their parents. This focus impacts the expectations placed on teachers and administrators as well as school policies and procedures. It also impacts the ways in which parents and community members interact with schools. Schools that serve children whose parents are high-status professionals operate accordingly by educating students to assume that status as well.

The idea that education is an item of value to be conferred upon children and that a quality education is something to be obtained, negotiated, and/or brokered by parents on behalf of their children is a concept that has been termed the educational endowment (Hill 2011). When education is treated as a commodity that can be endowed to future generations based on the wealth, efforts, and influence of their parents, the economic principle of scarcity is applied to the provision of education (Hill 2011).

Simply put, the economic principle of scarcity states that supply is limited while human demand is unlimited. There are only so many resources to go around. Because the demand is greater than the supply, the value of the good increases as does its cost. The result is that some individuals can afford the resource while others cannot. Under the principle of scarcity, there is increased competition for limited resources. The fact that one person or group of people receives the resource makes it less likely that another individual or group will be able to access the same resource.

Applied to schools, the principle of scarcity causes individuals to fight against or be resentful of programs, services, and resources that do not benefit their children but benefit others. This is because the provision of these programs, services, and resources has a perceived opportunity cost for the students who are not directly benefited by the program.

Thus, in an inequitable system, those who have access to greater resources will often fight against the provision of additional resources for others because they, sometimes correctly, believe that they will have to give up some of their resources to provide for others. This has frequently been seen in discussions about closing the achievement gap and improving educational equity.

Middle class and upper middle class families that have the resources to broker the best education for their children strategically select schools that provide the resources and experiences they expect to secure their children's place in society. Families that do not have these resources and families that trust schools to provide the quality of education that their children need often are not afforded the same kinds of educational resources and experiences in schools.

Even when school choice is widely available, spots in well-regarded public schools, charter schools, and private schools go predominantly to children whose families have greater financial and social capital and resources. Children whose families cannot or will not pay high school fees, attend numerous parent meetings, donate resources or raise funds for the school, complete a detailed application process, pay tuition (in the case of private schools), or complete similar tasks have a very low likelihood of getting in to the schools. Students from low-income backgrounds and students with disabilities or limited English proficiency who do get into the schools are much more likely to be expelled, drop out, or be counseled out.

The only way to ensure a high-quality, equal education for all of America's students is to ensure that there are public schools in every locality that are open for all children and provide the quality of education that every child needs and deserves. Private schools and charter schools can be very effective for some; however, the removal of resources from public schools to fund private and charter schools leaves the students who remain in public schools with a system that does not have the resources to provide an adequate education for all students. This adds to the current inequality of schools throughout the nation.

Recently, there has been much focus on the use of voucher programs to provide families with school choice. These programs provide parents with tax funds (i.e., vouchers) to pay tuition for public, charter, private, or parochial schools. Vouchers have been promoted as the way to allow families to access better schools than those that are available in their local community. By promoting school choice and competition, the argument goes, schools will improve as they attempt to compete for students. However, this ignores the economic realities of school choice.

Competition in education is a two-edged sword. Parents and families with the resources to choose among schools look for the best schools. These families have power over the schools because the schools want their children (and the tuition or funding that comes with them) to come to their schools. On the other hand, in a competitive model of schooling, schools also can choose among the "best" students and families.

This typically results in the "good" parents (i.e., those who have social and financial resources) getting the slots for their students while parents without money and other resources and parents whose children have special needs are left to send their children to schools that are under-resourced.

When one searches out the most highly regarded public school districts in the nation as well as the public schools with the greatest success at producing high student achievement, there are clear commonalities with regard to the resources and experiences provided in the schools.

Moreover, both parents and educators have a strong sense of what students need to be most successful in schools. Those with the knowledge and means to do so select schools for their children that possess specific resources, establish a specific type of environment, provide certain experiences, and achieve expected outcomes. Unfortunately, not all families possess this option.

Although much work has been done to set minimum proficiency levels and academic standards for students, very little attention has been paid to the need to identify societal goals and expectations for the educational experiences of all children in all schools. Setting expectations for equitable outcomes is necessary for ending failure as a default. However, setting expectations for outcomes without establishing expectations for inputs and experiences is ill conceived. We know the inputs that are necessary to achieve the desired outcomes. These inputs should be central to the conversation about improving student achievement and closing the achievement gap.

The quest for equity in schools must include a discussion of both inputs and outcomes. Although the argument for considering both inputs and outcomes as indicators of equality of educational opportunity was made back in James Coleman's 1969 report, providing equal and adequate experiences, resources, and expectations for all children has never been widely attempted in American schools.

Because education is greatly influenced by experiences, designing schools to afford students the necessary experiential curriculum is a prerequisite to closing the achievement gap. To produce schools designed for the success of all children, we must create and firmly establish a clear vision of what all children desire, need, and deserve from schools. That vision must represent a new fundamental right to public education.

The term "fundamental right" is important because it makes the allocation of resources, services, and programs enforceable. By nature, the quest for equitable schooling stands in opposition to the long-standing power structures of our society. As Frederick Douglass put it, "Power concedes nothing without a demand" (Douglass 1857). Recognizing the provision of a specific quality of education as a fundamental right allows those without power or influence to make a cogent demand through the courts if necessary.

What is or should be the specific vision of education for all children? The vision coincides with what most families and communities desire from schools and consists of six components that are necessary for widespread student success. They are academic preparation; classroom/school environment; exposure/experience and opportunities; expectation setting and horizon expanding; relationships and interactions; and ethical, social, and emotional development.

These components are fundamental to educating all children for life. Only by providing all children with these inputs while eliminating failure as a default can we make wholesale, meaningful changes to the long-term achievement gap.

ACADEMIC PREPARATION

Academic preparation is the aspect of schooling most frequently addressed by those interested in school reform and accountability. The meteoric rise and precipitous decline of the Common Core State Standards between 2010 and 2016 demonstrates the extent to which the topic of academic preparation is intertwined with politics. Education is a frequent topic in the political discourse on the national, state, and local levels. Typically, part of the discourse about education focuses on what all children should be taught while other parts of the discourse revolve around who should have the power to determine what students should be taught.

There seems to be a consensus around the desire for US public education to be the best and the view of reading, math, and science as the "basics" (harkening back to *A Nation at Risk*) on the national level. However, other priorities win out for families and communities at the local level. These priorities include a well-rounded education and the ability to be successful beyond elementary and secondary school.

To provide academic preparation inputs that are necessary for all students to succeed, our nation must ensure that all students receive:

- A comprehensive liberal arts education that includes knowledge and skills in fundamental areas, including language arts, math, science, social studies, and history. All students' educations must also include knowledge and skills to prepare them for community citizenship; economic participation and success; and civic leadership, including economics, civics, and social/ interpersonal skill development. In addition, all students need and deserve education that goes beyond the basics to include the arts, humanities, physical education, and global education. This includes instruction in art (production and appreciation), music (performance and appreciation), health and wellness, physical education, ethics, and one or more nonnative languages.
- Curricula that reflect college- and career-ready and/or professional standards. Alignment to these kinds of standards allows students to access postsecondary education, training, and a variety of careers and pursuits.
- Frequent exposure to and exploration of a wide variety of fields and trades. One aspect of failure as a default is the belief by many students, families, educators, and leaders that the career choices of groups of students are limited by their race, background, or culture. To change this belief, it is imperative that children from all walks of life gain true exposure to all the variety of careers, fields, and trades that are available for them to pursue. This should be included as a formal part of the curriculum beginning at the elementary level.

• Instruction in and practice with critical thinking, written expression, oral expression and argumentation, problem solving, reading and research, and design and creativity. These skills are typically missing from the curriculum of schools that serve low-income, African American, and Latino students, particularly if those schools have been labeled as failing. However, these are among the fundamental skills and habits that students must develop to close the achievement gap and achieve success.

Lack of clear, common academic guidelines about what students should know and be able to do combined with failure as a default result in substandard curricular expectations for students who are considered to be less able. This makes the adoption of and alignment with college- and career-ready standards and expectations for inputs critically important.

Traditionally, professional organizations of members of different fields and educators have created standards to indicate the exposure that students should have to their fields. The advent of NCLB put a damper on the promotion of these standards because states were focused intently and exclusively on state standards for reading and math. This left no room for professional standards for art, music, or other fields. In the future, however, our comprehensive liberal arts education should rely heavily on these kinds of standards to establish the appropriate breadth and depth of curricula outside of language arts and mathematics for all children.

CLASSROOM/SCHOOL ENVIRONMENT

Though infrequently discussed apart from discussions of school safety, the importance of the physical environment of classrooms and schools is undeniable. Classroom and school environments are designed in ways that reveal the underlying beliefs about children in the environment. The impact of building design and the maintenance and upkeep of facilities is widely recognized.

Many schools and districts have limited resources to maintain, improve, and update their facilities. As a result, many schools throughout the nation lack the facilities and learning environments that most middle class and upper middle class families take for granted.

Unfortunately, because schools in the United States are funded predominantly through local property taxes, low-income students, African American students, and Latino students are more likely to be educated in drab, rundown, old, and poorly designed facilities. Whether directly or indirectly, this negatively impacts student achievement.

Closing the achievement gap in American schools will require that every child be taught in school and classroom environments with:

- Safe, clean, well-ventilated, well-lit, climate-controlled classrooms
- Windows that allow outside light in
- Ample room for all students to have designated personal space
- Fixtures and furniture that are appropriately sized and designed for the developmental level of the children in the space
- All student spaces in close proximity and accessible to other classrooms to avoid isolation
- Bright, clean hallways and gathering spaces
- One or more gymnasiums with ample space for large group gatherings and physical activities
- Ample clean, well-lit restrooms that include stalls with doors for appropriate privacy and safety
- A school library with ample nonfiction and fiction books about a wide variety of topics and at a variety of reading and interest levels[2]
- Safety and security measures that are designed to blend into the environment
- Safe green outdoor spaces that are free from environmental hazards (e.g., toxic waste, power lines, lead, etc.)[3]
- Accessible technology, including computers, laptops, tablets, or handheld devices along with filtered high-speed wireless Internet access
- Colorful displays of student resources and work

In too many communities, schools serving low-income communities possess physical environments that communicate that failure is a default for students. Sometimes this is due to outside factors, such as schools' being located under power lines or near landfills. At other times, it is due to physical factors within the school, such as lead pipes and leaky roofs. Most commonly, however, it is due to the use of the physical environment. Both environmental justice and school design are pivotal to promoting the success of all students.

EXPOSURE, EXPERIENCES, AND OPPORTUNITIES

A fundamental part of the schooling process is exposure to new experiences and the provision of new opportunities. Student exposure builds students' vocabulary and background knowledge. It promotes their ability to interact in new and unfamiliar situations and settings. It builds students' confidence and allows students to see themselves as belonging in positive settings. In addition, each new experience provides the specific knowledge promoted in that setting. For example, when a student visits the local library, she or he learns about libraries but also gains access to the knowledge and resources that are available in the library.

Schools in middle class communities expose students to numerous experiences and resources that prepare them for future success. When students live in communities and attend schools that lack resources, they are at a disadvantage in school and beyond.

To reset the default to success, schools should ensure that every student receives:

- Exposure to local, state, and national cultural and natural resources, including museums, theaters, and national parks
- Travel to locations outside of their local community
- Easy access and frequent visits to well-stocked school and community libraries
- Safe community or school parks and recreation programs and facilities
- Exposure to civics and financial education
- Free and frequent access to computer technology and filtered Internet resources
- Participation in a wide range of cocurricular and extracurricular activities in the arts, academics, science, technology, leadership, personal development, career exploration, and sports. This participation not only affords students exposure and experiences, but it also has the added benefit of improving student engagement in school (National Center for Education Statistics 1995).
- Admission to advanced coursework tied to an outside standard of quality, such as International Baccalaureate (IB) and Advanced Placement (AP) or equivalent
- Safe and enriching programs for after school and school breaks that support the goal of increased exposure

Schools cannot replace the exposure that children receive in their homes and communities. However, the exposure provided in schools can make a meaningful difference in the kinds of experiences students have and the vocabulary, background knowledge, and setting-specific knowledge that students acquire. Exposure impacts current and future achievement.

EXPECTATION SETTING AND HORIZON EXPANDING

One of the most insidious aspects of failure as a default is the presence of long-term low expectations and narrow horizons for Latino students, African American students, and low-income students. As was discussed previously, these low expectations and narrow horizons impact all aspects of the design of schools as well as the many messages that students receive in schools.

An integral part of schools that are successful in creating positive achievement is the setting of high, appropriate expectations and the expanding of students' horizons. Students in these schools interact with adults who believe that they not only can but should be highly successful both in everyday assignments at school and in their future academic careers and life beyond postsecondary education. These expectations have a significant impact on the ways in which adults interact with students.

In the absence of these expectations of success, adults prepare students for a future that they expect to be limited by who they are, where they come from, how much money they have, or the specific circumstances of their lives. To raise student achievement and close the achievement gap, schools should provide all students with:

- Clear academic expectations grounded in the idea that students are smart, capable, and destined for success
- Broad curriculum options designed to maintain open options for higher education and training
- Exposure to adults from similar backgrounds and ethnic groups with a variety of careers. Never having seen a person like him or her in a field of study or career impacts a student's belief that that career is an option for him or her.
- Interaction with college students and college graduates in a variety of fields of study
- Interaction with students from different racial/ethnic groups, economic backgrounds, cultures, regions, and countries. More than ever, many stu-

dents attend schools that are racially, ethnically, and/or economically segregated. Success in the larger society requires that students be able to
interact comfortably, confidently, and compassionately with people from
different backgrounds.

• Access to specialized programs for talented students, including intern-
ships, leadership development programs, and camps

Low-income students, African American students, and Latino students seldom receive full exposure to the experiences that can broaden their horizons.
Even when these experiences are available, they very often require that families pay for them. This puts these students at a disadvantage compared to
their middle and upper middle class peers. To close the gap in achievement,
schools must eliminate the gap in expectations and broaden the horizons of
all students.

RELATIONSHIPS AND INTERACTIONS

The quality of relationships and interactions within schools is of critical
importance. Few aspects of schools have a greater impact on student comfort,
risk taking, growth, and motivation than the nature of the relationships between children and adults in and around their schools. This fact is seen in
schools regardless of the population of students they serve. However, it may
have an even greater impact on academic achievement for low-income students, African American students, and Latino students.

African American students, in particular, demonstrate a cultural belief
that the main driver of learning is the interaction between the teacher and the
student. Teachers are supposed to demonstrate personal authority and care
for the students (Hill 2011). When there is no relationship or a negative
relationship between teachers and students, learning is inhibited.

The importance of relationships and interactions is well known. However,
the quality of relationships and interactions in schools is seldom addressed as
a part of accountability systems because it is extremely hard to measure and
legislate. Although this may make relationships and interactions impossible
to meaningfully address at a policy level, this aspect of schooling is too
important to ignore. It must be addressed by educators and school leaders at
the local level.

To eliminate failure as a default and close the achievement gap, all students in every school must experience meaningful, positive relationships

with adults who are committed to their success. These kinds of relationships will be evidenced by interactions with these common characteristics:

- Warmth, caring, and empathy.
- Meaningful conversation between adults and children, including questioning. Educators typically spend most of the instructional day talking. Meaningful conversation with students requires taking turns and allowing students to help shape the conversation.
- Adults listening for student content, reasoning, and emotion.
- Opportunities for students to question the status quo and voice their opinions and arguments. The ability to voice dissent clearly, respectfully, and appropriately is an important skill in a democratic society.
- Meaningful responses to student questions.
- Polite, respectful tone and vocabulary in all situations.
- Disciplinary and management techniques that focus on clear communication, improving behavior, and maintaining relationships.
- Absence of verbal and nonverbal aggression (e.g., sarcasm,[4] sighing, shaming, eye rolling) (Glenwright and Pexman 2010).
- Absence of physical aggression and verbal or nonverbal threat of physical harm (including corporal punishment).

African American students, Latino students, low-income students, and boys of all backgrounds are more likely to have negative interactions and relationships in schools. This impacts school discipline and student achievement and contributes to the achievement gap.

ETHICAL, SOCIAL, AND EMOTIONAL DEVELOPMENT

A focus on ethical, social, and emotional development is severely lacking in our vision of public schools. For students throughout our nation, this emphasis is vital to individual, family, community, and societal success. Young children, particularly those who live in poverty, are routinely exposed to violence, aggression, anger, greed, and other character flaws through the media and in their communities. Today's schoolchildren have far more exposure to death within their communities than any other generation.

In 2016, fifty-two individuals were shot in Chicago on Mother's Day weekend. Three of those individuals were school-age children or youth. Children have been murdered on their way to school, coming home from school, walking to their grandparents' house, in the park playing basketball, and in many other places.

Even children who do not live in a community with high rates of crime or gun violence have been unduly exposed to and immersed in frequent and random violence. In 2012, a gunman with an AR-15 assault rifle and other guns entered Sandy Hook Elementary School, a school in a predominantly white middle class suburb, and murdered twenty first-graders and six teachers.

The nightly news routinely includes a rundown of individuals who have been attacked, murdered, or arrested. Media coverage shows protests over the killing of African American men and boys by police officers. Celebrities and other individuals routinely attack one another via social media. Political candidates seem to promote or condone violence, and the nation has been at war since before most current public school students were born.

In the 1950s, air-raid drills were a common activity that took place in elementary schools all around the country. Children were taught to duck and cover if they heard the air-raid siren. To help children and parents feel safe from the distant but massive threat of nuclear weapons, the government put out flyers, information, and cartoons to help people feel prepared to survive the threat of nuclear attack. Although duck and cover would not save anyone from a nuclear bomb, communities felt as though they could do something to protect themselves against a threat over which they had no control.

The twenty-first-century version of duck and cover is designed to protect against a threat from within. It is known as the lockdown or active shooter drill. In schools across the country, students, from three-year-olds in early childhood education to high school students and students on college campuses, routinely train and practice for the day that a maniac with assault rifles, handguns, and other weapons breaks into their school to kill them and their teachers and classmates. This is a sad state of affairs.

Perhaps even more sad is that students have come to accept these threats to their safety, security, and existence just as they have come to accept the fact that in many of their neighborhoods it is not safe to play outside, go to the park, or even sit on the porch. In this new reality for our students, it is no longer feasible to ignore children's social and emotional development or the development of strong character and true resilience.

Schools in every community must attend to the ethical, social, and emotional learning needs of children. Ethical, social, and emotional learning and support in schools should be characterized by:

- One or more professional social workers and/or counselors on-site.
- A school nurse or school health clinic available on-site.
- Direct social skills instruction beginning at the primary level and continuing through the start of high school.
- Crisis-intervention and student support.
- Ethics instruction grounded in common values.
- Constructive, positive discipline techniques.
- Cultural awareness instruction. Cultural bias is detrimental to the ethical and social development of individuals, families, communities, and society. Empathy and respect for those who are different from oneself is necessary for the future of democracy.

A lack of ethical, social, and emotional learning instruction has a negative impact on students in all schools. It may have a more significant impact on students in communities that have experienced more violence and a lack of resources.

Until schools provide equitable and adequate inputs and experiences for all children, gaps in student achievement outcomes will continue to exist throughout the system. Each successive generation that receives a substandard education is less likely to be able to broker a high-quality education for the next generation. This has the potential to create a doom loop for US educational, cultural, economic, and political exceptionalism. It is time to provide all children (regardless of the perceived merit earned by their families) with the inputs that are commonplace and expected as part of a high-quality education by those with the resources to select the best school settings for their children.

In the second part of this book, we will consider factors that educators and leaders can address to have the greatest impact on eliminating failure as a default and closing the achievement gap. We will look specifically at each of the main elements of the experiential curriculum—structures, messages, attitudes, and beliefs.

NOTES

1. The widespread use of property taxes to fund public education has contributed to a general acceptance of the idea that a quality of one's school is determined by one's address. Since housing is often segregated along racial, cultural, and socioeconomic lines, the prevalence of schools that predominantly serve one group of students is as high as it was in the 1969

Coleman Report. The fact that the vast majority of Americans have only witnessed this arrangement provides support for the idea that this arrangement is only a natural result of individual merit.

2. The American Library Association no longer publishes standards for the number of books per student. However, the average is twenty-seven books per pupil at the elementary level and sixteen books per pupil at the high school level. For more information, see www.ala.org/.

3. A discussion of environmental justice as it relates to schools would require an additional book. I have visited schools with playground equipment directly under power lines as well as schools dangerously close to industrial waste.

4. I have had numerous arguments with well-meaning educators about the use of sarcasm with children and adolescents. Most children do not understand sarcasm until they are around ten years old, and even then, they regard it as unkind or insulting. I regard using sarcasm as not worth the threat it poses to educator-student relationships.

II

A Long Time Coming

Chapter Five

Structuring Success

"Liberty trains for liberty. Responsibility is the first step in responsibility."

—W. E. B. Dubois, 1909

Structures are powerful. In schools, structures shape much of the experiential curriculum. Indeed, structures are the element of schooling in which teachers, staff members, and administrators are most thoroughly engaged and empowered. School improvement and school reform are focused on structures within classrooms, schools, districts, and communities more than anything else.

In addition to shaping student experiences, school structures also send clear, but unspoken, messages about educator priorities. School leaders learn, early on, that things that are noticed, measured, recognized, and structured are the things that get done. Things that are discussed but not built into the structures of a school or district seldom become part of a school's or district's culture.

Because structures are created by educators, leaders, and policy makers who have been immersed in failure as a default, the structures in schools often serve to perpetuate the achievement gap even as educators, leaders, and policy makers work to improve achievement for all children. The structures that have the greatest impact on the achievement gap include those revolving around reading instruction, student discipline, written curriculum, intervention and services, personnel, and decision making.

READING

One afternoon, I visited a fifth-grade classroom for their read-a-thon, a marathon reading event in which the last half of the school day was devoted exclusively to reading independently. At the invitation of the teacher, the students raised their hands eagerly, hoping to be selected to "whisper read" to me as the VIP visitor in the room. The teacher chose Salesha. She strode over confidently with her chair and book and sat next to me at one of the student desks.

After introducing herself, Salesha told me the title of her book (a collection of short fables and folktales), and she suggested that we start reading the next story, titled "Bruh Buzzard." I agreed and Salesha began whisper reading in what turned out to be more than a whisper. It was clear by her pace and careful articulation that Salesha was trying hard to read fluently and articulately for my entertainment.

The story revolved around a vulture who was taunting and tormenting the master of an old mare who was getting close to death. The vulture told the man that the mare would soon become the vulture's food. When Salesha was about three paragraphs into the story, I interrupted to ask, "Do you know what a buzzard is?" Salesha replied with an unconcerned no. I had suspected that this was the case because although Salesha was reading articulately (for a nine-year-old), she displayed a flat affect with little vocal expression even as she read the disturbing parts of the text.

Next I asked, "Do you know what a vulture is?" Again, my whisper reader said no. At that point we stopped to talk about how vultures feed on the carcasses of dead animals and that the word "buzzard" is another name for a vulture. The discussion brought a slight look of horror across Salesha's face as she uttered a quiet, "That's gross!" She now realized that Bruh Buzzard was waiting for the old mare to die so he could eat her. The story now had meaning (although not a pleasant one). We finished the story and I thanked Salesha for reading with me.

I walked away inspired, as I always am, by the tremendous potential bound up in a young child. At the same time, I felt consternation knowing that this young girl's education to this point made her so confident and eager to put on a show demonstrating her reading skills that the fact that she lacked the understanding of the basic elements of the story did not matter.

Clearly, Salesha could articulate that she did not know what a buzzard was. Did we fail to teach her that meaning matters? Did we communicate to her that it is inappropriate to stop to ask questions? Have we made sounding like a reader more important than being a reader?

Reading skills are fundamental to success at every level of schooling and to effective functioning in society. It is for this reason that politics have long surrounded the teaching of reading skills. One of the first limitations placed on oppressed groups is a prohibition against their learning to read, acquiring reading skills beyond a rudimentary level, and/or reading certain materials.

This has applied to women and girls, who in some parts of the world, still are not educated. It has applied to enslaved African Americans who were legally barred from being taught to read. It has also been applied to rural, urban, and suburban people in poverty, whose access to reading instruction and reading materials has been limited.

At the elementary school level, reading instruction not only consumes most of the school day and school year, but it also consumes much of the discourse around curriculum and instruction. The preeminence of reading continues into middle school and high school, as students' access to the curriculum is increasingly tied to their reading skills.

No structures have a greater impact on the existence and perpetuation of the achievement gap than the structures surrounding reading instruction in schools. Not only is reading a basic skill that is fundamental to all instruction in schools, but it also depends on many other skills that are vital for effective functioning in modern society. As a result, the ability to read effectively remains a major predictor of school success and a main determinant of success or failure in civic life.

The reading achievement gap is pronounced as early as first grade, and in many cases, it grows throughout a child's years in school. By eighth grade, the gap between the proficiency percentages of African American students, Latino students, and low-income students and white middle class students is 26 points, 24 points, and 24 points, respectively.

The structures that surround reading instruction provide evidence of educators' beliefs about the students being taught. These structures also demonstrate educators' knowledge of and misconceptions about teaching reading. Reading instruction may focus on the rudimentary processes of decoding while neglecting the higher-order and critical-thinking skills of comprehension and analysis.

Alternatively, reading instruction may revolve around comprehension, analysis, and critical thinking while also addressing foundational skills. A focus on low-level reading skills is often found in schools, classrooms, and programs that serve low-income children, African American children, Latino children, children in urban areas, and children with disabilities.

In schools with well-meaning educators, students' struggles with learning to read effectively often lead to instructional practices that only serve to further limit students' progress and instructional practices that focus on helping children appear or feel successful by sheltering students from high academic demands. This takes the form of:

* Removing actual reading from reading instruction
* Placing excessive focus on decoding and fluency while neglecting comprehension and vocabulary
* Withholding comprehension instruction and exposure to complex texts for students who are below grade level
* "Helping" students by giving them answers, hints, and clues so they don't have to struggle, take risks, or get answers wrong
* Limiting exposure to authentic print, text, and vocabulary to avoid confusing students
* Focusing instruction on getting students to recall information about pieces of literature instead of analyzing and thinking critically about texts
* Indiscriminately providing students with reading material that is below grade level

In settings where large numbers of students struggle with rudimentary reading skills or come to school behind their white middle class peers, these instructional practices and curricular structures often make up the planned curriculum for the school. Students progress through a reading curriculum that was planned for students who struggle and perpetuates and widens the achievement gap by focusing on low-level skills.

Because educators work largely in isolation from other schools, the educators within a school, the students themselves, and their parents rarely grasp the extent to which they are disadvantaged by both the planned and delivered reading curriculum. However, when standardized tests display a comparison between reading achievement in these schools and reading achievement in middle and upper class schools, the disparity is staggering. Moreover, instead of shrinking the disparity between groups of students, the reading interventions of schools often serve to maintain, or worse, to increase the gap that is already seen at the start of kindergarten.

Reading instruction in all schools should be purposefully designed to combat failure as a default and bring about success for all children. Educators and school leaders should take the following steps to build structures around reading instruction that support success for African American students, Latino students, and low-income students.

Provide direct foundational reading skills (i.e., phonemic awareness and phonics) instruction to all children at the primary grade levels as a part of the core curriculum. The foundational reading skills of phonemic awareness and phonics are often treated as though they are necessary only for students who struggle to learn to read naturally. Educators assume that students develop these skills at home before coming to school or that they simply pick up these skills as they are exposed to written language in the school setting.

It is this assumption that leads to the neglect of foundational reading instruction to all students. The students who do not need this instruction to become proficient readers are not disadvantaged from receiving this instruction. On the other hand, when schools do not provide foundational reading skills instruction, the students who need direct instruction in phonemic awareness and phonics to become proficient readers are sometimes irreparably harmed.

Phonics and phonemic awareness instruction should not be reserved for students who struggle. Instead, this instruction should be an integral part of reading instruction. The skills of blending sounds and syllables and identifying and differentiating sounds are skills to be used in both reading and writing. Phonics skills begin with letter-sound correspondence and progress to "sounding out" words in reading and writing, to recognizing syllables and word parts.

Direct instruction should be incorporated into the curriculum daily. Teachers should model the use of these skills in reading and shared writing. Students should be taught to use these skills as they write independently. Students should be held accountable for demonstrating the skills they have practiced.

When assessing phonics and phonemic awareness, educators should remember that the skills have no long-term value in isolation. What should be assessed is the students' ability to use the skills for word attack while reading and writing.

Provide daily instruction on comprehension skills and critical thinking using complex texts for all children beginning in kindergarten. Educators can build listening comprehension skills using texts that are above students' inde-

pendent reading levels. Educators should select texts that are complex, vocabulary rich, and of high interest for students. Then, they should engage
students in listening to, discussing, reflecting on, and responding to what is
read.

Students routinely develop listening comprehension skills at a rate that
outpaces their development of decoding skills. At any given point in their
primary and intermediate schooling experience, most students have the capacity to comprehend language that is at a higher level than their reading
levels. It is critically important that schools take advantage of this discrepan-
cy and develop comprehension skills beginning when students start school.

Comprehension instruction should include identifying the who, what,
when, where, in what order, and why of the text so students can get a basic
understanding of a text. Effective comprehension instruction will then take it
to the next step. It should include developing an understanding of the tools,
purpose, and point of view of the author.

Finally, comprehension instruction should include the process of analyzing, reflecting, and incorporating new information into what students already
know or have experienced. This last component is most often the one missing
from instruction in schools because it is not measured.

A teacher's approach to teaching comprehension also matters. A common
mistake when teaching comprehension skills to students who struggle is
attempting to teach high-level skills in a low-level way. Students may learn
the definition of making inferences or analyzing the author's purpose by
listening to a presentation and taking notes. However, to acquire these skills,
students must engage in applying them before, during, and/or after reading.

*Assign all instructional duties in reading to licensed teachers with train-
ing in teaching reading.* School leaders must provide training for teachers
who have not had it, are not proficient, or who do not feel comfortable with
teaching reading. They must not rely on teacher education programs to provide the only training on teaching reading. Most teacher preparation programs provide minimal training on teaching reading, and, in most cases,
preservice teachers receive no instruction on meeting the needs of students
who struggle with reading. This leaves the important work of teacher training
on reading instruction to individual schools and districts.

Educators who are new to teaching or new to a school or district should at
a minimum receive training on the use of the school's or district's reading
program/curriculum resources. All educators should also be provided with
more global training on the process of learning to read and on the identifica-

tion and treatment of reading difficulties. Reading instruction training should be provided to every educator regardless of assignment, with more extensive training being provided to every educator with responsibility for reading instruction and/or core academic subjects.

Educators who are responsible for reading instruction should be trained in the best practices of teaching all aspects of reading. Schools should universally apply these best practices and monitor them to ensure that each student's experiential curriculum includes consistent engagement in high-quality reading instruction.

Volunteers, parents, and paraprofessionals can provide valuable help to engage students in reading. Focus volunteer, parent, and paraprofessional reading work on supplemental reading experiences, reading mentoring, and reinforcement. Their activities should include modeling reading skills, reading aloud to emerging readers, reading with students in small groups or one-on-one, and discussing what is read with students.

Essentially, the role of volunteers and paraprofessionals should be focused on practicing what the student has been taught during core instruction and helping students become independent readers. Volunteers, parents, and paraprofessionals who have received appropriate training can also assist by accompanying students and counseling them on book selection.

By lowering the student-to-adult ratio, volunteers and paraprofessionals can allow students to engage with the text and an adult. The paraprofessional or volunteer can encourage or prompt students to stop and think about aspects of the text, make connections to what they are reading, make inferences, draw conclusions, and assimilate new knowledge. It is important that the volunteer or paraprofessional interact as an equal partner with the student, taking turns during discussions and promoting student thought and talk. Working with a volunteer or paraprofessional should be a supplement to (not a replacement for) core reading instruction.

Ensure that all students participate in core reading instruction with the teacher in the classroom. When students need additional instruction, practice, or intervention, educators should provide it outside of core reading instruction time. It is a common impulse to remove students who struggle from core instruction for them to receive separate instruction "at their level." The unintended consequence of this is that students lose access to the grade-level curriculum and the ability to appropriately converse with their peers on the topics included in core instruction. In addition, this structure ensures that students who struggle with skills such as decoding and fluency also develop greater deficits in the areas of comprehension and vocabulary.

Core reading instruction typically includes whole-group instruction that includes introducing specific themes, vocabulary, genres, and decoding and comprehension skills. In many cases, core reading instruction also includes some form of small-group instruction in which activities are differentiated for groups of students.

All students can benefit from engagement in core reading instruction. When students have difficulty decoding the grade-level text, educators have had success with making accommodations and differentiating instruction to allow students to access the curriculum. In this process, it is important to plan differentiation based on the specific needs of the students. For many students, decoding grade-level text is a challenge. However, they can engage with and comprehend what they hear, and they can engage in and contribute to class and small-group discussions. Writing may be a struggle, but they have ideas that they can communicate.

Frequently and routinely engage students in reading, comprehending, and responding to a large number and wide variety of texts. Wide reading improves students' comprehension, background knowledge, and vocabulary in ways that cannot be replaced by direct instruction or drill and practice. Since many African American, Latino, and low-income students need additional background knowledge and vocabulary to succeed academically, frequently reading a variety of texts is even more important for them.

Engagement with reading, comprehending, and responding to texts should not be limited to the reading curriculum or to the classroom setting. Reading experiences (including being read to) beyond those in the classroom setting are necessary to promote students' reading skills. This includes after-school and summer reading programs, reading mentor programs, and independent reading. It also includes providing students with access to and engaging them in reading a large collection of books. This should come in the form of large, diverse classroom, school, and community libraries. To the extent possible, it should also include home and personal libraries.

In the past, the American Library Association has recommended that schools provide access to a specific number of books per student in schools. This recommendation has been changed to simply note the importance of access to "a well-developed collection of books, periodicals, and non-print material in a variety of formats that support curricular topics, and that are suited to inquiry learning and users' needs and interests" (American Library Association 2016).

Engage students in writing frequently to monitor and assess their individual understanding, thinking, and communication. In the absence of written responses, it is extremely difficult to ensure that each child engages in critical thinking in response to questions. Students who do not know the answer, do not feel comfortable taking a risk, lack self-confidence, or simply do not enjoy the subject or topic can avoid engaging in oral discussions altogether by simply waiting for others to chime in. Routinely engaging students in writing down their thoughts, reflections, arguments, evidence, and justifications allows educators to review each student's learning.

Children also benefit from taking on the role of the author. Students should be frequently engaged in writing about their ideas, reflections, feelings, and aspirations. It is important for students (particularly those who are reluctant writers) to associate writing with speaking. It is another way to communicate one's thoughts. Writing should not be limited to a weekly writing project or a daily journal entry, nor should all writing be graded.

Provide small-group reading instruction that is differentiated to the needs of students as a part of core reading instruction throughout the elementary grades at a minimum. Small-group reading instruction, or guided reading, is a fundamental part of elementary reading instruction. During small-group reading instruction, students are placed in groups of four to six students for lessons that include reading from texts that are at their instructional reading level, practicing decoding skills, and applying comprehension strategies. Teachers take the time during small-group reading to provide students with individualized attention. This allows the teacher to notice student thinking and errors and to focus on the specific needs of students.

Teachers frequently assess each student's reading level, progress, and ability to apply new skills. They use this information to form and modify the groups to ensure that students are continually challenged and to plan instruction. This level of daily, individualized attention is a necessary component of core reading instruction for all students.

When schools provide only whole-group reading instruction, fail to appropriately differentiate small-group instruction, or neglect to provide the instruction necessary for students to move through reading levels, all students suffer. However, that suffering is often most pronounced for students who have traditionally been victims of the achievement gap.

Attend to the teaching of vocabulary. Vocabulary instruction should in-clude direct instruction on words and word parts, vocabulary strategy instruc-tion, identification of vocabulary in context, and exposure to and discussion of new vocabulary. For many educators, vocabulary instruction methods mir-ror spelling instruction. Teachers give students a list of vocabulary words to memorize prior to a matching, multiple-choice, or fill-in-the-blanks test. The vocabulary words are those included in the curriculum guide or a word list or selected randomly.

To meet the needs of students who need additional vocabulary develop-ment, schools should directly teach important roots and affixes and academic vocabulary. However, vocabulary instruction must not stop there. In addition to directly teaching, modeling, and requiring the classroom use of academic vocabulary and word parts, educators should teach, model, and engage stu-dents in the use of vocabulary learning strategies that will allow students to analyze the meanings of words and phrases in text and speech and to acquire new words as a part of their personal receptive and expressive vocabulary (Allen 1999).

When students struggle to learn how to read, engage in the struggle with them. Students who do not learn to decode as rapidly as other students quick-ly become the outliers in the class and school. They suffer from ever-growing isolation, as they find that they cannot participate in discussions and activ-ities in the class, they can be easily identified by their peers, they are unable to interact socially with their peers, they are separated (i.e., "pulled out") from their peers for reading instruction, their teachers are frustrated with their lack of progress, and their families are at a loss for what to do. This isolation serves only to increase and make seemingly insurmountable the gap between students who struggle and students who excel. Isolation is further exacerbated when students recognize that other students like them are experi-encing the same predicament.

When students struggle, they often find that teachers and other adults begin to disengage from them. This is the opposite of what students who struggle need. Teachers may begin to ignore students who struggle. They avoid calling on them to answer questions, ignore their disengagement (e.g., daydreaming or sleeping in class), rush them when they speak or ask a question, or give them the answers or say never mind and allow them to do nothing when they do not know what to do. When students believe trying does not work or is not noticed and when students learn not to take risks, many make silent agreements with teachers that they will both quietly disengage.

When students struggle, teachers must specifically take steps to engage with the students as individuals. For most students, this should include an age-appropriate discussion of the student's strengths and struggles and the plan of how the teacher will help the student to grow. It is important for educators and school leaders to recognize that they are responsible for creating an effective plan to build the student's reading skills. That responsibility cannot be placed on the shoulders of families or the students alone. If the teacher does not know how to help the student, she or he should consult with expert reading teachers and/or do research to develop a plan to meet the student's needs.

Educators and school leaders can help students by setting specific goals with the students who struggle and by identifying for the students what they can do to help meet the goals. Instead of simply assessing the students, educators should include the students in the assessment process and teach the students to self-assess. It is important that educators recognize students' efforts and celebrate their progress while continuing to set challenging goals for the student.

When students struggle to learn to read, there is a reason. Identify and address it. As a first-grader, a young African American boy was identified as needing reading intervention. He seemed to have at least average intelligence, but his reading rate was well below the benchmark. As a result, his reading comprehension, as measured by his ability to answer comprehension questions at the middle or end of the story, was significantly behind.

The worried parents came to me concerned about their child's reading skills. At their request, I sat down to read with the charming, well-behaved six-year-old to try to determine the reasons for his difficulty. As we sat together, the child began reading. He read the first three words in the sentence before averting his eyes to look at the picture on the page. He examined the picture, talking about minor details in the illustration, such as the color of the character's hat and the presence of a bird in the tree.

Then he resumed reading at the fourth word and read two or three additional words before again averting his eyes and telling me about an obscure connection he had made to a word, phrase, or illustration in the story. By the time he finished reading a sentence, the child had no idea what the sentence was about, and things would only get worse as he moved from sentences to paragraphs to pages.

It took about ten minutes to teach the first-grader that periods (and other punctuation) were important and to establish a rule that he could not stop reading to look at the pictures, make connections, or make comments until he reached a period. We practiced this for a few sentences and then filled the parents in on the new rule that would apply anytime their son was reading to or with them.

With a little coaching, the parents continued the rule at home during their school-required twenty minutes of reading per night. At my instruction, within a couple of weeks, they had modified the rule from stops being allowed at the end of each sentence to stops being allowed at the end of each paragraph and, finally, to stops being allowed at the end of each page. Suddenly, the child who had been identified for reading intervention became a proficient reader.

It is important not to assume that the cause of difficulty with learning to read is a lack of intelligence or a learning disability. In most cases, difficulty with learning to read is related to limited experiences with phonemic awareness, vocabulary, and/or text or lack of access to appropriate, consistent, effective reading instruction.

Cognitive impairment has a powerful impact on the ability to learn to read texts. However, it is important to note that cognitive impairment is a low-incidence disability that cannot account for the magnitude of the achievement gap. In addition, specific learning disabilities in reading tend to be overidentified based on the quality and consistency of reading instruction children receive in schools. Diagnosed learning disabilities in reading, such as dyslexia, impact many students. Unfortunately, very few educators have received training to teach students with dyslexia.

Reading assessment by fully trained educators is critically important to determining the source of reading difficulties. When students are identified as struggling with reading, educators should make a practice of individually assessing them in a realistic reading situation to identify skill deficits or gaps.

Continue teaching students to read throughout elementary and middle school. Continue monitoring reading-skill development in high school. Many educators, school leaders, and policy makers subscribe to the mistaken belief that children learn to read in grades K through 3 and read to learn in grades 4 and up. Educators and school leaders must work against this myth.

If students stop learning to read at the end of grade 3, they will be functionally illiterate as adults. The reality is that successful students in grade 4 and up continue to learn to read higher-level texts. They continue to build their reading vocabulary and learn new comprehension skills. In most schools, nonfiction reading is neglected in the primary grades. As a result, many students begin learning to read nonfiction, informational texts in the intermediate and middle grades.

Schools should continue to teach reading and monitor skill development throughout the middle grades to ensure that students are able to apply critical-thinking skills to their reading. Schools should also continue to promote or require independent reading for all students beyond the required readings that typify middle school and high school English classes. Students who have struggled with reading in the past and students who have had limited access to reading materials frequently stop reading by fourth or fifth grade if schools shift their focus away from reading instruction.

DISCIPLINE

When I was an assistant principal working in a high-poverty school that serves primarily African American children, I unleashed a controversy among the staff members at the school when, on the first day of school, I refused to suspend a student for inappropriate behavior on the bus on the way to school. After the buses arrived, a fourth-grade boy was brought to the office with a note saying that he had violated the school zero-tolerance policy for physical aggression.

After investigating the situation, I found out that the boy had gotten into a wrestling match with his sister while on the school bus on the way to school. When they got off the bus, the boy and girl chased each other on the sidewalk around the school. When the teacher discovered what had happened, she brought the child to the office with the expectation that he would be suspended for violating the zero-tolerance policy.

After speaking with the boy about the incident, I, ignorant of the school's zero-tolerance policy, contacted the boy's parents; let them know what happened; assigned him a detention; and made him write a letter of apology to his sister. Then, I promptly sent him to class.

Five minutes later, the teacher arrived in the office with the boy in tow. She sat him down in the outer office and proceeded to tell me, in front of the child, that he was not allowed to come to her classroom, that he had violated the zero-tolerance policy, and that he was to be suspended. She went on to say that the teachers at the school had worked very hard to establish the zero-tolerance policy and that I had no right to try to change it. So this young boy's first introduction to his teacher this school year was hearing his teacher state that he was not welcome or allowed into her classroom.

The establishment and maintenance of school and classroom discipline is fundamentally important in schools. Discipline structures have an intense impact on the experiential curriculum. This is particularly the case for low-income students, Latino students, and African American students, who receive a disproportional share of the disciplinary actions in schools.

In the quest to provide discipline, educators and school leaders often establish disciplinary structures that have a disparate negative impact on youth for whom failure is a default. Educators and school leaders should strive to create classroom and school environments in which the need for disciplinary actions is minimized and such actions are used only to address misbehavior and not for simple cultural misunderstandings.

Proactively teach and model the behaviors desired and expected of students with the understanding that students need to know what is expected of them. Educators and school leaders have specific, detailed expectations for student behavior and interactions. These expectations cover every area from how students move to the words they use, from the volume of their voices to how they ask questions and register dissent. These, and many other aspects of human behavior, are inextricably tied to culture.

The problem for educators, school leaders, and their students is that educator and school leader behavioral expectations go unexamined and unarticulated. Because the expectations are cultural and seem natural to educators and leaders, the assumption is made that everyone knows and subscribes to the same expectations.

As a result, when students behave in ways that do not meet the expectations, their actions are seen as noncompliant, disrespectful, inappropriate, aggressive, or antisocial. This is often the case even when transgressions of the expectations are minor, such as talking too loud, interrupting, failing to make eye contact, or making too much eye contact (e.g., staring too long or too intently).

To meet the needs of a diverse population of students, educators and school leaders must both examine and articulate their expectations and beliefs about student behavior and discipline and build structures around discipline that will promote student learning and combat failure as a default. When examining their expectations, educators and school leaders must differentiate between the expectations that are necessary in a school setting and those expectations that are unwarranted, unrealistic, unfair, or simply a matter of personal or cultural preference.

Only expectations that are necessary to promote learning and build the school community should be articulated, directly taught, and maintained. Educators and school leaders should operationalize these expectations by teaching students the expectations and parameters that should be followed in each setting. All educators, leaders, and staff members should support and adhere to the agreed-upon expectations.

Directly teach students the verbal and rhetorical codes that indicate behavioral expectations and directives. Verbal and rhetorical codes are cultural in nature. It is important that educators not make assumptions about how students communicate. Particularly when there is a difference in culture between educators, school leaders, and students, misunderstandings and miscommunication can abound.

For example, in schools serving middle and upper class students, it is common to hear a teacher say, "Let's have a seat," instead of giving students the command to "Sit down." Students who are used to receiving a command may misinterpret the teacher's words as merely a request or as an option that is being presented to them. The intent behind the teacher's words is a command even though the phrasing and tone do not indicate this.

In some schools, educators and school leaders go to the opposite extreme. They phrase every request or statement as a forceful command that would easily be interpreted by most adults and virtually all professionals as highly disrespectful. Students in these schools emulate the verbal and rhetorical codes that have been routinely used with them. When they communicate in the same way with peers or adults in the school or community, their behavior is seen as disrespectful as well.

Educators and school leaders should strive to communicate with respectful words and in a respectful tone with all students and use direct commands only when necessary based on the situation. In all schools, they should teach students what different verbal and rhetorical codes mean as well as how and when to communicate using them.

When consequences are necessary, plan disciplinary actions to serve as consequences instead of punishments. Select actions that do not sabotage relationships or future academic success and behavioral progress. Disciplinary actions that destroy relationships between students and their teachers and peers serve to increase the likelihood of future misbehavior. In addition, disciplinary actions that involve removing a student from instruction help to create learning gaps from which students struggle to recover.

When planning overall school discipline systems or individual disciplinary actions for student conduct, educators and school leaders should specifically consider how a student will be reintegrated and return to good standing within the classroom and school community. This may include the use of restorative justice practices as well as postdiscipline conferences with the student to reengage the relationship as the student returns to class.

Reintegration and reengagement are critically important when a student has been removed from the classroom environment for a time. In these cases, it is common for the student to experience a high level of anxiety in addition to any anger or shame she or he may possess because of the situation that caused the disciplinary action. It is not uncommon for the educator, school leader, and/or students in the school or classroom to experience anxiety and negative feelings as well. Educators and school leaders must handle reintegration thoughtfully to avoid undue tension, fear, and other triggers of inappropriate behavior.

Reentering a classroom having missed a significant amount of academic work and instruction can also cause great anxiety in addition to causing low student achievement. Many schools and districts, prompted by laws aimed at reducing the school-to-prison pipeline, have made it a practice to allow students who are suspended or otherwise removed from class to continue doing their coursework for credit. This is an important step. However, it is not enough. Educators and school leaders should also consider student academic progress and a student's ability to catch up with missed instruction as a part of reintegration plans for students.

Involve trusted adults early and often. Engage the village at all stages of the school-discipline process. Relationships with parents and families are critical to maintaining discipline for all students. Educators should make a habit of beginning to develop relationships with families long before the need for disciplinary actions arises. This process should include individually contacting families and providing them with information about what students will be learning, what expectations teachers will have for students, and how teachers make sure that students learn.

When behavioral concerns arise, educators should contact families right away before behaviors escalate to the point of warranting significant disciplinary actions. Often, contacting a parent or guardian is reserved for one of the last steps on the ladder of disciplinary actions. However, if educators involve families appropriately, a parent contact can serve to address behavior before it escalates.

The African proverb "It takes a village to raise a child" has become a cliché in schools and communities today. However, when it comes to maintaining strong student discipline while also maintaining strong relationships with students, this proverb still applies.

For many African American students, Latino students, and low-income students, the concept of family goes far beyond a nuclear family made up of one or more parents and children. The idea of family often includes an extended family of grandparents, aunts and uncles, pastors and religious leaders, family friends, and neighbors. These family members play important roles in children's lives and upbringing. With the consent of parents or guardians, educators and school leaders can use these extended family relationships to create a supportive village for children.

Directly instruct students on the way to meaningfully, appropriately, and effectively register dissent and advocate for themselves. Self-advocacy is an important skill in our society as is the ability to appropriately disagree and fight for what one believes. One frequent source of student misbehavior is a student's perception that he or she is being treated unfairly or unjustly or that an educator does not like or care about the students. When students feel as though they are being mistreated, they experience a natural urge to fight back. For African American students, many boys, and some other groups of students, fighting back against oppression or perceived victimization and saving face are cultural values and expectations.

Educators and school leaders should not attempt to suppress a student's tendency to confront situations she or he believes to be unfair or unjust. Instead, educators and school leaders should recognize that there will be times when students need to express disagreement or dissent and advocate for themselves. Educators and school leaders should actively teach students appropriate methods for communicating when they believe they are not being treated appropriately. This instruction should begin before students are in a difficult situation.

When a situation arises in which students express a need to advocate for themselves or their interests, the educator or school leader should try to step back from the situation and counsel the student on ways to communicate his or her feelings and reasoning. It is important for educators and school leaders to fill students in about the process that will be followed and any recourse they have if they disagree.

This knowledge will not only assist the student with the specific situation, but it will also carry forward to help the student apply self-advocacy skills in the future. Educators and other adults can help students develop the skills by role-playing different situations, by analyzing ways in which people in history have appropriately voiced dissent, and by rehearsing what a student will say and how he or she will communicate his or her needs.

Establish clear expectations for your own behavior using your students' reactions and expectations as one of your guides. A difficult, yet critically important, task for educators and school leaders is the task of setting behavioral expectations for themselves and one another. Although they are professionals who generally dislike conflict and work diligently to meet the needs of students, educators and school leaders are human beings with specific communication and behavioral patterns that impact their students, families, and colleagues.

Occasionally, educators and school leaders engage in behaviors that are problematic for some of their students. Usually, this happens because the educator or school leader simply does not notice how his or her behavior can impact or trigger the emotions and behavior of those around him or her.

Educators and school leaders should consider the strengths, needs, characteristics, and personalities of the students in their classrooms and schools and use this information to set shared expectations for the behaviors of adults throughout the school and school system. Behaviors that communicate a lack of caring, that trigger negative behaviors in students, or that have a negative impact on student learning should be identified and eliminated. Examples of these kinds of behaviors would include using sarcasm, shaming students, showing clear favoritism for a student or group of students, or behaving in a threatening or intimidating manner.

CURRICULUM

Leanna Randall graduated as valedictorian of her high school class in a large, urban school district. With dreams of being a doctor, she had completed the school's AVID program and achieved a perfect high school GPA. She took every math and science course that was offered to her at her school. She completed several honors and Advanced Placement (AP) classes, including AP science courses.

As she approached the end of her high school career, she began applying to colleges and going on college visits. She fell in love with the large state school atmosphere and selected a school that had an outstanding pre-med program.

Because Leanna had graduated at the top of her class and she was a minority student from a low-income background, she qualified for numerous scholarships and grants to allow her to pursue her dream of becoming a doctor. Leanna packed her things and went off to the university knowing that she would need all her dedication and tenacity to reach her goal.

Just two months later, Leanna was stressed out and in danger of losing her scholarships. You see, during her four years of high school, despite taking all the math and science classes that were offered to her, despite taking numerous AP courses, despite participating in the AVID program, and despite graduating at the top of her class with As in every single subject, Leanna had never completed a lab course while in high school.

Although she had taken the highest level of math afforded to her in high school, she had never experienced applying the math concepts in a scientific or other real-world context. She had read about and studied science, but she had never designed or completed a high-level experiment. She had never gathered authentic data or completed written lab reports.

Without these experiences and the corresponding skills, Leanna entered college-level math and science courses that required a prerequisite of knowledge that she simply did not have. On the first day of classes, she was already behind. Educators at other schools had taught, encouraged, and/or forced students to apply their high-level math knowledge to science, statistics, and real-world activities.

The other students in the pre-med program had all graduated at the top of their classes. They had all taken honors and AP courses. They all received As throughout high school. However, unlike Leanna, they had done these things at schools that provided numerous high-level science lab courses. They had done so in schools that exposed the students to conducting experiments; required students to complete weekly or sometimes biweekly lab reports; expected students to apply high-level math skills to science; and promoted reading, writing, and analysis.

Through no fault of her own, this intelligent, hard-working, talented African American woman was forced to struggle to play catch-up to achieve her lifelong goal. She had done everything in her power in high school, but she was handicapped by a system that told her that she was successful but did not prepare her to succeed outside the confines of her poor, low-achieving urban high school.

One of the key determinants of student learning is the scope and quality of curriculum provided in schools. When schools do not provide instruction or courses in areas that students need, students are often helpless to gain exposure to those curricula. In many schools, curricular areas that are untested are eliminated either purposefully or through neglect.

In some cases, schools choose not to offer particular curricula based on community preference or educator assumptions about the instruction students want or need. Even within curricular areas, educators and school leaders make decisions that impact the scope and quality of the curriculum in specific schools and classrooms and for specific children.

Children learn from exposure and experience. Decisions such as not offering high-level courses, not offering lab experiences, not engaging students in research and writing, and not teaching or using academic vocabulary are common in schools that lack resources as well as schools struggling to improve standardized test scores. Each of these decisions impacts student learning and access to future opportunities.

Provide a curriculum that includes all subject areas for all students. The focus on tested subjects during the school accountability era has resulted in the narrowing of the curriculum in many schools that struggle to meet student test-score goals. In too many schools, students do not routinely receive instruction in science, social studies, writing, and other areas. This puts them at a disadvantage throughout their school careers and closes off student options, such as pursuing postsecondary education and careers in STEM fields. Unfortunately, the additional time focused on reading and math typically does not significantly raise student achievement those areas.

School leaders and educators should review the curriculum at all schools and all grade levels to identify curricular areas in which students receive little or no instruction. It is important that the review focus on the instruction that students actually receive instead of simply reviewing the curriculum guide or other documents. This is necessary because some narrowing of the curriculum happens without planning due to time constraints and educator or school leader preference.

If the review shows that students are not routinely receiving focused, high-quality instruction in reading/language arts, writing, mathematics, science, and social studies as well as specialized instruction in other areas, such as the arts, health and wellness, and physical education, school leaders and educators should implement a curriculum adoption or writing process to move toward providing a complete curriculum. The curriculum adoption or writing process must include having educators and school leaders commit to the implementation requirements for each curriculum.

For example, when writing or adopting a science curriculum, educators and school leaders should provide guidance on questions such as:

- What is the daily and weekly instructional time allotment for each grade level?
- What chapters/units/sections are required?
- What specific strategies and methods should be emphasized? For example, all classes should participate in at least one experiment or investigation during each chapter/unit.
- What specific tasks will be required of students at each grade level? For example, all seventh-grade students will write lab reports for each experiment.
- What parts of the curriculum should be assessed?

Similar questions can be applied to writing, social studies, and other curricular areas.

School and system leaders should also review the age and practical usefulness of curriculum resources for all curricular areas. When curricular materials are more than nine or ten years old, they have often reached the end of their usefulness, and educators begin to replace the adopted curriculum with other materials to fill the void. School and system leaders should create and implement an ongoing curriculum renewal process and schedule that ensures that students receive high-quality instruction in all curricular areas.

Plan curriculum for maximum flexibility for future options, including high-level and specialized courses. When schools make curricular decisions, they are also making decisions about the future options that will be readily available to their students. Some schools limit students' options by limiting the course subjects, course levels, and specialized programs that will be offered to groups of students or in the entire school.

Many middle and high schools serving large numbers of low-income students do not offer honors or AP courses or courses in areas such as foreign language. If they do offer such courses, the courses are often limited in scope or limited to certain students. While schools in middle class and wealthy communities may offer fifteen different physical education courses, five or more languages, and twenty or more AP courses, this range of options is seldom available to African American students, Latino students, English learners, and low-income students.

While curriculum options in schools may be limited based on funding, educators and school leaders should ensure that they do not create additional limitations because they do not believe students are interested in or capable of participating in a wide range of programs and options. Educators and school leaders should plan course offerings based on the range of future options they want to see for their students. This should include providing students with access to high-level coursework that is tied to an outside standard of performance such as Advanced Placement and International Baccalaureate courses.

Beyond simply providing access to challenging, high-level coursework, educators and school leaders should support the participation of low-income students, Latino students, and African American students in these programs. In many schools, these students are drastically underrepresented in these programs. To promote and support their participation, educators and school leaders should look beyond traditional methods of identifying students for specific courses, personally invite students to participate, ensure that students are enrolled in class sections that include other students like them, and provide scaffolding for students as they adjust to the new level of expectation.

While it is a fact that not all students will go to a four-year college or university and not all students will enter a career in engineering, law, etc., school and system leaders and educators should plan each school's curriculum so that students will have the option to pursue those or other postsecondary paths. Educators should ensure that they do not limit students' options or force them to choose their path in elementary, middle, or early high school by limiting the school curriculum or the students' options.

Include writing and research as a formal part of the curriculum. Neglecting writing and research in elementary, middle, and high school curricula has a significant negative impact on student success in college and careers. In many cases, these skills are integrated into instruction in other areas. As a result, when students do not receive instruction in these areas, they often do not realize they have skill deficits until they struggle on college entrance exams, in college courses, or in careers.

Educators and school leaders should specifically address the inclusion and integration of writing and research skills instruction in each curricular area beginning with shared writing and research in kindergarten and progressing in rigor and complexity. As educators and school and system leaders renew and review curricular areas, they should create expectations for the ways in which all students will be engaged in writing and conducting research in the subject area. This includes subjects that are not traditionally writing- or research-intensive courses, such as mathematics and the arts.

INTERVENTIONS AND SERVICES

On a Tuesday afternoon, a seventeen-year-old high school senior asked to meet with the principal of his large, comprehensive high school. He had some time to talk because he had asked his football coach for permission to be late to practice. The principal always took the time to talk with students, so he asked the young man to come into the office and make himself comfortable.

The young man sat down and pulled his latest report card out of his bag. He showed the principal his straight As. When the principal congratulated him on his grades, the young man shook his head.

He explained that he had done everything he had been told to do. He had worked hard, done all his homework, studied hard, aced all his tests, and learned everything he was taught. He was in the process of completing his fourth year of English and math. He had completed three years of social studies and science. He worked hard and played hard for the team. But he had just received a letter informing him that, after review of his transcripts, the university that was recruiting him to play football and offering to provide him with a full-ride scholarship for four years had decided to rescind its offer.

Although the young man had done everything he was told, he was not eligible to play football at the university because the high school courses to which he had been assigned as a student with an Individualized Education Plan did not qualify for college admission and athletic eligibility.

His 4.0 GPA in special education classes meant nothing. If someone had only explained it to him, he could have taken "regular"-level classes with appropriate accommodations. He might not have received straight As, but even with a C+ average, he could have been prepared to take the next step. The young man's question for the principal was simple, "Why didn't anybody tell me?"

Unfortunately, this is not a unique story. Students who struggle in school are routinely provided services and interventions in schools. In many cases, these services are structured in a way that negatively impacts the student's growth, achievement, and future options. When failure is a default, educators and leaders often believe they are doing the best thing for students by striving for short-term gains. In these situations, it is easy to underestimate the impact poorly structured interventions, remediation, and special services can have on a student's future options.

School leaders and educators should take great care to ensure that the interventions and programs they design and implement do not inadvertently harm student achievement or limit student success in the long term. They should review all intervention programs and services and take the following steps.

Minimize or eliminate parallel curricula in which students have no hope of converging with the grade-level curriculum. Educators and school leaders commonly develop programs and curricula to address the needs of students who struggle with specific skills. The goal of these programs is typically to provide the students with focused instruction and intervention to eliminate skill deficits.

When school leaders and educators conceive of and plan programs and curricula for this purpose, it is imperative that they think strategically about ways to ensure that students served in the programs continue to build the skills necessary to take part in the grade-level curriculum. A separate program does not help the student in the long term if it precludes the student rejoining the grade-level curriculum. The curriculum plan must include specific steps that will be taken to accelerate student growth and learning and to provide students with exposure to the skills and accommodations they will need to be reintegrated into the grade-level curriculum.

When the program is instituted, educators and school leaders should closely monitor student progress to determine whether the plan is working in practice. They should review the progress of individual students and ask themselves, "What percentage of students in the program are successfully developing the target skills and reentering the grade-level curriculum?" Future programmatic decisions should be based on this evaluation.

Provide interventions and services in addition to (not instead of) the core curriculum. Students who struggle with learning benefit from additional instruction and time. One problem that limits the effectiveness of interventions in schools is the tendency to simply replace core instruction with remedial instruction. The result is that students who were struggling to learn while receiving grade-level instruction receive the same amount of instruction at a lower level.

Instead of using this approach, educators and school leaders should plan interventions and services that will allow students to benefit from more instructional time. By providing both core instruction and interventions, educators and school leaders have a greater likelihood of increasing the rate of student growth and learning. Schools can do this by providing interventions outside of core whole-group or small-group instructional time.

For example, educators can provide interventions before or after school and during independent classwork times. In addition, at the elementary level, interventions can be scheduled during small-group instruction and center times. In this case, the students would participate in the small-group instruction that is part of the core curriculum with the classroom teacher. Then, the students would participate in another intervention group with the interventionist, special education teacher, ESL teacher, etc.

At the middle school and high school level, some schools have accomplished this by providing students with double blocks of reading or English and math. The double-block courses provide students with additional instructional time. In addition, in many schools, double-block courses are cotaught by a content teacher and a special education teacher, ESL teacher, or other specialist. As a result, students receive additional time and focused, specialized instruction.

Monitor interventions and change or eliminate those that do not accelerate growth. Educators and school leaders sometimes become so focused on selecting and implementing intervention programs and services for students who struggle that they neglect to plan to evaluate the effectiveness of the intervention. A key idea when devising and implementing intervention programs is the understanding that assignment to an intervention program should not be permanent. If students never outgrow the intervention, it is not effective.

When students are assigned to an intervention group or service, educators and school leaders should identify the specific goals and success indicators for the intervention. Then, they should assess the effectiveness of the intervention programs and services to determine whether the target students are growing at a faster rate than they were without the intervention. Prior to selecting an intervention for a student, educators and school leaders should also consider whether the intervention program or service is the intervention option that will maximize a student's growth.

Educators and school leaders should not only monitor and evaluate the effectiveness of an intervention for individual students, but they should also analyze the overall effectiveness of each intervention program and service. If intervention programs that are implemented consistently and faithfully do not produce accelerated growth for students after an appropriate evaluation period, they should be replaced with interventions that produce greater growth.

Involve middle school and high school students in the decision making about their education. When adults gather to discuss the interventions and services that will be provided to students with learning needs, academic struggles, or disabilities, it is critically important that the students be involved in the process. This should include developing an understanding of their strengths and needs, their role in the process, and participating in setting and monitoring goals for their progress.

It is understood that children may not have the final say about aspects of their schooling, but they should be taught to understand the process and take part in advocating for themselves. Although this may be done (as required by law) for older students with Individualized Education Plans, adults often make significant educational decisions without involving adolescent students who struggle with reading or other subject areas, receive English learning services, have social or emotional needs, or receive other interventions and services. These students have no opportunity to advocate for themselves or provide input regarding their needs.

By the time students enter seventh grade, they should be given the opportunity to learn how decisions are made on their behalf. They should be allowed to provide input on areas that are appropriate for discretion, and they should be taught the difference between areas that are at the discretion of educators, parents, and students and those that are required. For example, a student cannot opt out of learning to read, participating in physical education, or passing a test on the US Constitution. However, he or she can give input on things like the kinds of study methods that will be used with him or her, which accommodations may be necessary, and what options may need to be available if he or she is struggling emotionally on a particular day.

Communicate with parents and students the consequences of the educational decisions made on behalf of students. In many cases, families and students do not know enough about the school system or curriculum to be able to understand or predict the long-term consequences of educational decisions made on behalf of students. Although educators and school leaders may also struggle to predict the impact of their decisions, it is important that they engage families and (when appropriate) students in that discussion.

What is the likely result of making this decision? What is the process the school is planning to follow? What concerns may this decision raise for the future? How will educators monitor the effectiveness of this decision? At what point can this decision be changed, by whom, and by what process? These questions apply to many educational decisions, including special education decisions, English learning decisions, course placement decisions, and decisions about retaining a student in grade.

African American families, English-learner families, Latino families, and low-income families are disproportionately left out, excluded, or allowed to opt out of discussions about educational decisions. As a result, many do not learn of the impacts of educational decisions made by school staff until it is too late. This promotes a lack of trust in educators and school leaders. To combat this, educators and school leaders should actively pursue meaningful conversations with families of all students receiving interventions and/or services at school.

For English language learners, provide instruction to support them in becoming fully bilingual and biliterate. In many schools, having a native language other than English is still seen as a disadvantage. Students who are English learners are immersed into English-speaking classrooms and provided a small amount of English as a second language instruction. Educators are expected to get students to stop speaking their native language and begin speaking, listening, reading, and writing in English as rapidly as possible.

The result of this approach is that English learners often lose out on the opportunity to become fully bilingual. In addition, because they are not afforded the opportunity to build their skills in their native language, they often underperform in all their academic areas. Their advantage of potentially being bilingual is turned into a disadvantage.

Whenever possible, schools should provide bilingual education programs for English learners who are native speakers of other languages. These programs should provide students with instruction in both languages and involve helping students to build their literacy skills in their native language. When this is not possible, educators and school leaders should provide instruction that is respectful of students' native languages and their English learning needs. It is important that all educators participate in training that will give them an understanding of language acquisition and effective methods for teaching and supporting English learners.

PERSONNEL

Over the past twenty years, Ms. Sutter has worked in every school in the district. She has been assigned to grades 1 through 6. She has been a Title I teacher, a writing teacher, an in-school suspension teacher, and a classroom teacher. Approximately every two years, Ms. Sutter was moved or reassigned until she finally landed at EFG Elementary School.

EFG was the poorest school in the district. Most of the students lived in the local housing project, and for fifty percent of them, English was not their first language. Teachers seldom, if ever, requested to go to EFG. The staff consisted of teachers who were new to the district, teachers who, like Ms. Sutter, landed at EFG after being bounced from school to school, and the occasional "true believer," who believed working with EFG students was her or his calling.

Ms. Sutter did not particularly care for working at EFG. Most of her students struggled with reading and received low test scores in math. She most often described her work at EFG as "crowd control." Ms. Sutter told her students, "I am here to teach the students who want to learn. For the rest of you, I get paid whether you learn or not." Other teachers seemed to work magic with these kids. Ms. Sutter supposed that it must be because they have the "good" groups of students.

Few structures have a greater impact on student learning than the structures around school personnel. Educators and school leaders wield a great deal of power over the experiential curriculum of every student in a school system. Excellent teachers can improve both the learning and the lives of students regardless of their backgrounds or needs. Those who enter the education profession are overwhelmingly noble, caring, and committed to student learning. School and school system structures related to personnel can assist or hinder a school's ability to attract, support, and retain excellent teachers and school administrators. School and system leaders should assist schools in the following ways.

Make teacher retention/tenure decisions based on the idea that tenure is a school- and district-shaping thirty-year commitment. Each year, school and system leaders in most states must decide whether to retain educators and school leaders and, after some legally prescribed length of service, whether to grant them tenure protections based on their performance. Much thought should be put into these decisions.

The appropriate emphasis can be placed on these decisions if school and system leaders assume that the teacher being awarded tenure is going to become a part of the school and district for approximately thirty years and impact the lives of hundreds of students for at least a generation. School leaders should make the process of awarding tenure an active one instead of allowing a teacher to achieve tenure by simply deciding not to leave a school or district.

In addition to considering an educator's proficiency with managing a classroom and planning, implementing instruction, and assessment in the classroom, school leaders should assess an educator's work ethic, commitment to meeting the needs of all children, ability to continue professional growth, talent for teaching, contribution to the school's professional community, and impact on the school's climate to determine whether she or he should be awarded tenure.

In some cases, school leaders feel compelled to retain a teacher because of his or her positivity and involvement in the school despite his or her lack of proficiency with planning and instruction. However, this is just as detrimental to student growth and achievement as retaining a teacher who has instructional skills but lacks the other necessary qualities.

The same level of scrutiny should be applied when making school or district leader retention decisions. It is less common for school or district leaders to be granted tenure protections or to stay in the same school or district for thirty years. However, leaders still have an indelible and long-term impact on schools and school districts.

Those charged with making employment decisions about school and system leaders should give strong candidates three or more years to shape a school or district. Along the way, consider both the leader's managerial and political skills and her or his ability to lead others to improve student learning; promote excellent teaching and services for all children; select, support, and evaluate staff and make effective retention decisions; and create and support a school culture in which every child is valued, challenged, and guided to success.

Assign teachers to students and students to teachers strategically to achieve the maximum achievement for all students. In many schools, students whose parents have the knowledge and means to demand the most-revered teachers are given the priority when teacher and class assignments are made. This is understandable because these parents are more likely to be vocal about their expectations and to complain if their children are placed with teachers who have a less than favorable reputation.

What this means for low-income students, African American students, Latino students, English learners, and students whose families are not willing or able to engage with schools in this way is that their needs are placed at a lower priority than students with more advantages. If school leaders want to combat the achievement gap, they must stop assigning these students to teachers whom school leaders know to be ineffective.

When educators and school leaders consider classroom assignments, they should aim to create classes that will make all students as successful as possible. School leaders and educators recognize that each teacher has his or her unique personality, strengths, needs, and way of doing things just as is the case for students. Instead of assigning students and teachers randomly or following parent requests and then assigning students whose parents did not make a request to the newest or least preferred teacher, school leaders and educators should assign students and teachers to one another based on what is known about their individual personalities, strengths, and needs.

Reserve teacher support (e.g., instructional coach, team leader, department chair) positions for educators with outstanding teaching skills and a talent for leading adults. Teacher support positions require educators to not only possess strong teaching skills and pedagogical knowledge, but they also require educators to possess strong leadership and communication skills as well as a willingness to work with adults. Not every strong teacher can fulfill this role.

If educators without strong leadership skills are placed in these roles, they are often rapidly overwhelmed with the demands of working with adults with different viewpoints, personalities, and agendas. Many find it difficult or impossible to make decisions or take actions that their colleagues may not like. They can either become isolated from other educators or paralyzed to take actions with which others disagree. In either situation, these educators are ineffective at improving teaching and learning.

Instead of selecting educators for teacher support positions based on their seniority, tenure in the district, or desire to do the job, school and system leaders should award these positions to educators who are most able to handle the demands of the job, including guiding decision making, building professional relationships, training and supporting others, advocating for students, and building consensus and commitment. When possible, school and system leaders should ensure that teacher support positions are not permanent and that educators may move into or out of those positions as appropriate.

Establish meaningful ways for excellent teachers to advance without leaving the classroom. One troubling aspect of the teaching profession is that there is so little opportunity for excellent veteran teachers to advance without ending their teaching careers. When teachers are ready to advance to a higher-level position, they often end up leaving or being removed from the classroom for an administrative position. As a result, classrooms and schools are continually robbed of some of the most-effective teachers.

This not only negatively impacts students in classrooms, but it also negatively impacts excellent teachers who want to advance but would rather not stop teaching. It is important to note that the talent and skill set that is needed to be an excellent school or district leader is somewhat different than the talent and skill set needed to be an excellent teacher. Some adequate teachers become outstanding administrators, and some outstanding teachers become only adequate administrators.

School and system leaders should allow excellent teachers to advance while remaining in the teaching profession. School and district structures that may allow for this include lead teacher assignments in which a teacher is selected to serve as the leader and support for a team of teachers; teacher mentoring programs in which an excellent veteran teacher provides mentoring and professional development for one or more novice teachers; professional development school partnerships in which excellent veteran teachers are observed by and provide practicum experiences for preservice teachers; and curriculum selection/development/writing programs in which excellent veteran teachers take on leadership roles in evaluating and improving curricula used by them and their colleagues. [1]

Specifically recruit and select the best educators available for every position without exception. The importance of hiring and assignment decisions warrants focusing significant effort on recruiting a number of quality candidates for each teaching, leadership, and staff position in a school or district. In some cases, current educators in a school or system are assigned to a position for a host of reasons other than being the best candidate. When school leaders fail to invest time in the recruitment process, they can easily end up having to select from a very small list of candidates or having to simply hire the only candidate available.

African American children, Latino children, low-income children, English learners, and students with disabilities are harmed the most by being taught by educators who lack the skills, willingness, or talent to teach well. To meet their needs, school and system leaders must actively recruit and select educators for their desire and ability to teach the school's students effectively.

Instead of asking, "Can this person do the job?"[2] school and system leaders should ask themselves, "Can this person do the job better than every other person I can find?" This question should apply to candidates being considered for hiring into the school or district as well as current staff members being considered for new assignments.

NOTES

1. For these options (or any others) to be advancements, they must be appropriately compensated.

2. This question has allowed nepotism and charity hiring in many schools and districts.

Chapter Six

Messages

In a small school district serving elementary school children in poverty, the superintendent led a gathering of all the school and district administrators and team leaders. The full-day meeting was focused on identifying students to be served through the district's Response to Intervention (RtI) program. The teachers and administrators soon began to discuss the many challenges they were facing—student attendance was low, parents could not help at home, student mobility was high, some students' behaviors were a concern, time was limited, etc.

They said, "*These kids* don't have enough respect. *These kids* don't know how to think. When they set these standards, they didn't think about *these kids*." Then, they began discussing the tests.

In the state where the school district operated, schools were responsible for the scores of students with Individualized Education Plans (IEPs) who were served in different schools. As a result, the school had low scores for students whom the educators had never even met. Moreover, students with IEPs in the district received few services in the classroom, and teachers had not been trained and felt as though they did not know how to support them.

As that point, the director of special education took the floor. She said, "The law stipulates the services for *my special ed kids*. You don't need to worry about them. You all should focus on what you need to do for *your gen ed kids*. *My* kids will be taken care of."

Chapter 5 explored the power of structures and noted that many structures also send messages to those within the school community. In this chapter, the focus is the messages that are sent when educators, leaders, and policy makers speak, write, and make and communicate decisions.

Both formal and informal messages in and from schools have a powerful impact on student achievement and growth. Educators, leaders, and policy makers send messages even when they are not trying to. They send messages to their colleagues and other staff members in schools that help to shape the culture of the school.

They send messages to community members about schooling and education policy. They send messages to families about the expectations, priorities, and beliefs they have about students. And they send messages to students about their values, priorities, and beliefs about students and their communities.

Messages sent within and from schools are strongly influenced by the social, economic, and political dynamics of society. The power structures, beliefs, and biases of the larger society are often mirrored within schools. School leaders, educators, staff members, students, and families bring their experiences into schools with them. When they speak, write, and otherwise communicate, these individuals reflect societal dynamics.

Messages that are sent in schools are important because they communicate about the culture of the school and the community. Educators, staff members, and school leaders are often rapidly indoctrinated with the attitudes and beliefs that are prevalent in a school. The way people talk and communicate, what they say, and how they say it has an impact on everyone in the system. The culture of a school or school system is perpetuated because each new staff member, student, or family that enters the system is assimilated through the messages they receive in or from schools.

To gain an understanding of the impact messages have on failure as a default and the perpetuation of the achievement gap, one should consider the words that are used in schools; the planned messages that are sent within and from schools; the unspoken signals that communicate culture, expectations, and beliefs; and the areas of silence or lack of communication. Each of these elements of the messages sent in and by schools is important to understanding how educators, school leaders, and policy makers inadvertently communicate failure as a default.

THE POWER OF WORDS

The language that educators use is extremely powerful. The words that educators use to describe or to plan their work can both reveal and shape their attitudes and beliefs about education, the students, their families, and their communities. Words can also send clear messages to colleagues, staff members, students, and families. Take, for example, the language of individual ownership—"my" and "your." Each time these words are used in an educational setting, they expose the sense of ownership held by educators.

An attitude of ownership can be beneficial when the sense of ownership is shared among all stakeholders. However, in schools and other organizations, the language of ownership can often communicate a sense of separation and an attitude of self-interest. It sends the message that educators and school leaders are concerned only about students, families, staff members, etc., that they identify as belonging to them.

Another kind of message of which educators must be aware involves the language of objectifying children. Language that objectifies children has the effect of dehumanizing them and lumping them into groups. An example of objectifying language is using the modifiers "these" and "those." At times, educators can be heard using phrases like "these kids don't," "those kids can't," "these kids need," or "those kids will." The use of "these" and "those" indicates that the group of students are in some way inherently different from the norm. It sends the message that students are not a part of "us."

A similar message is conveyed when individuals refer to others in dehumanizing group terms such as "the Blacks," "the Hispanics," "minorities," "Mexicans," and "free lunch kids." These terms often precede messages that describe a large number of individuals as a monolithic group that is inherently different and separated from the speaker. Educators, school leaders, and policy makers should be aware when they begin a statement with these words that their message is likely to communicate stereotypes and bias.

The high-stakes testing that came along with the No Child Left Behind Act added new language to educators' vocabularies. This troubling language includes words and phrases like "bubble kids" and "kids who count." It also includes otherwise harmless language such as "subgroup." The messages sent by these terms and phrases are problematic because of the policies to which they are connected in many school environments.

"Bubble kids" is the term used to describe students who are "on the bubble," or within a few points of reaching proficiency on a high-stakes test.

"Kids who count" is the term for students whose scores will be used in determining proficiency levels for school accountability. "Subgroup" is the label for a group of students with a common characteristic by which their test score data is disaggregated. A subgroup must include a minimum number of individuals to "count" toward school accountability measures.

All these terms send the message that the learning of some students is more important and valuable, while the learning and performance of other students is not a priority. This message is particularly clear when educators and school leaders choose to provide extra services for "bubble kids" and "kids who count" while neglecting the needs of students who score far below the proficiency benchmark and those whose test scores will not impact school accountability.

Other language that sends messages about educators' attitudes toward students include such descriptors as "low," as in "my low kids," and "high," as in "my high kids." Similar labels such as "IEP kids" or alternatively, "special ed kids," "slow learners," etc., both communicate and strengthen specific attitudes and beliefs. Using these and other labels sends the message that the identified group of students is different from other groups while also being a monolithic category of students.

Of particular concern is the language and attitude of otherness that can often be detected when educators refer to poor, African American, or Latino children. These include labeling students and families in veiled racial or ethnic terms. For example, sometimes individuals use terms such as "urban," "at risk," "illegal," or "kids from _____" (insert the name of a low-income neighborhood). Each of these has a negative racial, ethnic, or socioeconomic connotation in most settings.

Alternatively, sometimes individuals use terms that are perceived as code words for white middle class students, such as "good" (as in "schools need to pay more attention to the good kids" or "schools should listen to the good parents"), "hard working," "gifted," and "mainstream." In this case, the message received by students, families, leaders, and colleagues is that some students are the "other" and cannot be expected to succeed at the same rate as white middle class students.

PLANNED COMMUNICATION

In October, the annual ritual began. Newspapers all over the state ran front-page stories about the latest release of statewide standardized test results and

Adequate Yearly Progress (AYP) designations for local public schools. For the third year in a row, the news report stated, ABC School District failed to make AYP. Three subgroups—the black, Hispanic, and IEP subgroups—did not make AYP. As a result, the district was labeled as failing to make AYP. As the only local school district with subgroups and the only local district not meeting the standards, ABC School District received all the media attention.

Pressed by numerous phone calls requesting interviews, the superintendent issued a press release. It stated that the district was being held accountable for "the performance of traditionally underachieving subgroups." The superintendent went on to explain that the district was full of "good schools" and was identified as failing because African American students, Latino students, and special education students performed poorly on the tests.

The newspaper printed the story. From that point on, community members were keenly aware of three messages:

- ABC School District was the worst district in the area because it served too many of "those" kids.
- "Good schools" fail because of African American students, Latino students, and special education students.
- African American students, Latino students, and special education students can be expected to perform poorly on tests.

Each year since the passage of the No Child Left Behind Act, school and system leaders have been faced with the task of explaining school accountability results, test scores, and AYP labels to newspaper reporters, community leaders, business community members, politicians, families, and school staff. And every year, the applicable test scores, school accountability results, and AYP labels in schools and systems across the country have shown a persistent achievement gap that has resulted in schools across the nation being labeled as failing schools.

Moreover, every year, schools that have served large numbers of African American students, low-income students, Latino students, and English language learners have demonstrated poor overall performance on school accountability tests when compared to schools serving white middle class students. Schools throughout the nation have prepared press releases, statements, and letters for various audiences attempting to explain the presence and perpetuation of the achievement gap.

Many times, the planned communication that is sent from schools reflects the culture of the school and the policies about students and student achievement that is prevalent in the educational community. As a result, they often reflect the idea that failure is a default for students that are considered to be disadvantaged by their backgrounds, identities, native languages, disabilities, and home lives.

When school leaders, system leaders, and policy makers discuss or make presentations about schools, they commonly preface their remarks by describing the schools of which they speak. This description inevitably begins with a discussion of the school's demographics and location. It goes something like this: "I am superintendent of XYZ School District in _____. We serve _____ students in grades K–12 in _____ schools. _____ percent of our students qualify for free or reduced lunch. _____ percent of our students are limited English proficient." "Our school is predominantly black and Hispanic" or "We are a high-achieving school district."

These statements send the message within the profession and to those listening from outside of the profession that the racial, ethnic, and socioeconomic demographics of a school or district are a significant part of what defines the school or district. It also communicates the work being done in schools and districts should be viewed through the lens of the identities of the students they serve.

Another source of messages that may communicate failure as a default is a school's or district's mission statement and statements of belief. Creating mission statements and statements of belief is a common practice in schools. When educators and school leaders create their mission statements and statements of belief, they often reveal their aspirations, fears, and perceived limitations. It is common for mission statements and statements of belief to include several caveats and conditional statements.

While they may reflect the desired reality of the school community, mission statements and statements of belief can also communicate a lack of responsibility being accepted by educators and school leaders. The following are examples of a school mission statement and belief statement that demonstrate this.

"Our Mission: Working together with parents, business, and the community, _____ School District will strive to promote lifelong learning, citizenship, creativity, and innovation in a caring, professional environment."

"All students can learn . . . " This statement is concluded with one of several qualifiers from "to their potential" or "at their own pace" to "when parents and educators work together."

Statements such as these send the message that the expectation for student learning is conditional. The school's mission is not directly related to student learning. The school can be successful in achieving its mission even if some or all students never achieve success. The belief statement about the ability to learn is qualified as well. The qualifiers that are listed are commonly accepted, but they also send a message. If students can learn to their potential and at their own pace, who determines the limits of the students' potential or the appropriate pace of learning? If students can learn when parents and educators work together, what happens when they do not?

UNSPOKEN SIGNALS

There is a saying that goes "It's not what you say. It's how you say it." An important lesson for school leaders is the idea that what an individual means is not as important as what she or he says and what an individual says is not as important as what she or he communicates. Unspoken messages can be some of the most powerful messages students, families, and community members receive from schools. These messages are often not meant to convey the ideas that are gleaned from them.

One kind of message that can communicate loudly even though it is unspoken is a message about who belongs in a particular school, class, program, or setting. Take, for example, gifted or honors programs. It is quite common to find gifted programs and honors programs in schools that serve students from a variety of backgrounds. Frequently, these specialized programs are predominantly filled with white middle class students who have resided in the community or attended the school for many years.

Low-income students, African American students, Latino students, English learners, and students who are new to the school are often unrepresented or underrepresented in these programs. On the other hand, these same groups of students are often overrepresented in special education, remedial programs, and disciplinary settings. This sends an unspoken message to students regarding where they belong.

Other messages that can be sent without words include low academic or behavioral expectations, lack of care or concern, and frustration with or feelings of futility regarding student learning and achievement. Low academic or behavioral expectations are communicated by allowing students to quit or produce work they know to be substandard or deciding not to expose students to specific activities because they are challenging or require higher-order thinking or executive-functioning skills.

Lack of care or concern is communicated by ignoring verbal or nonverbal requests for help, by showing what is perceived to be favoritism toward other students, or by failing to display adequate effort to improve student learning. Frustration with or feelings of futility regarding student learning and achievement are communicated by giving up when students seem to have difficulty mastering a skill right away.

SILENCE IS DEAFENING

Another way in which the message that failure is a default is sent is by neglecting, avoiding, or resisting communication on specific topics or with specific groups of individuals. Families who have ample resources and families who live in middle and upper class communities demand and receive a great deal of information about the workings of the school and district, educational policies, school and district programs and services, and even personnel.

More importantly, they demand and receive a great deal of information about everything that impacts their children, from classroom happenings to their children's progress, and from assessment results for their children to what teachers plan to do to ensure their children's success.

On the other hand, low-income families, African American families, Latino families, and nonnative English–speaking families often receive incomplete information from schools because they do not have the resources to demand all the information they need. Communication with these families is often limited to required information and information about problems or concerns. In many settings, educators and school leaders choose not to communicate complete information with some families.

For example, in many settings, educators display a fear or apprehension of communicating negative information to African American parents, Latino parents, and low-income parents. This fear may be the result of past experiences that educators have had or stereotypes of members of these groups. This fear may also stem from hearing stories about the experiences of others. Whatever the reason for the fear, it causes a lack of communication with families that results in families not receiving the information they need to support their children's education or play a meaningful role in educational decisions.

In some cases, educators decide not to communicate information with parents as a favor to their students. They make a spoken or unspoken deal with the students in which they commit not to share negative information with a student's parent or family member if the student commits to behaving appropriately or completing homework or if the student pleads with the educator not to. This sometimes reflects the educator's or school leader's fear or lack of understanding of the family's culture and/or discipline practices.

For some parents and families, educators and school leaders neglect to provide information to families in a language they can understand. Many schools have a population of students whose families are nonnative speakers of English or who do not speak English at all. Educators and school leaders in many schools send home flyers, newsletters, report cards, assessment results, and other communications in English only, thereby ensuring that nonnative English speakers miss out on the information that is provided.

Neglecting to provide families with the information they need by communicating in their native language or providing translation sends a clear message that the school values English only and that educators and school leaders do not care enough about sharing information to provide the information in a language that is accessible to families.

To ensure that they are not sending the message that failure is a default, educators, school leaders, and system leaders should monitor and strategically change the messages they send in the following ways.

Review all planned communication for the messages sent to different individuals and groups. School and system leaders should build a network of individuals with different backgrounds who can review letters and press releases and provide input and feedback regarding the messages that may be sent through the planned communications. Leaders should consider the messages that will be perceived by students, families of different backgrounds, community members, and others who have little or no direct connection with the schools.

Beware of labels. It is human nature to want to name or label people and phenomena. Unfortunately, labels typically oversimplify the characteristics of people and phenomena and tend to lump individuals together in ways that can discourage considering individual needs. Used inappropriately, labels can also serve to dehumanize people and send a message of otherness.

These impacts of using labels are particularly detrimental in schools because children are especially susceptible to the messages sent through labels. School leaders and educators should strive to become comfortable with the idea that each student is a unique individual with unique strengths and needs. Research can provide rough information about groups of students, but to meet the needs of all children, educators and school leaders must look past the labels and demographics and focus on the individual.

Whenever they use labels to speak about children, educators and school leaders should think about the message that the label sends. If an educator speaks about planning for her "low kids," does the label limit her or his flexibility of thought regarding the group of individuals being discussed? When a school leader starts a discussion about the needs of the "special ed" students, does the label help educators make effective decisions about curriculum and instruction?

Always assume a child is listening when speaking about him or her directly or indirectly. One of the most harmful assumptions educators and school leaders make is that students do not hear, pay attention to, or understand the things that are said about them. This assumption is extremely damaging because not only do students hear and pay attention to the things that educators and school leaders say about them and other students like them, but they also understand what educators and school leaders say in a specific way.

Students rapidly come to view as contempt the things educators say about them when they think they are not listening. Once they believe that educators and school leaders hold them in contempt, students view any statements of caring as pretense and deceit. Moreover, they are likely to internalize the attitude about their ability and achievement that they hear from their educators and school leaders in spite of themselves.

Remembering to always speak as though the students and families are listening helps educators combat failure as a default in two ways. First, it eliminates the potential that students will hear educators and school leaders saying things about them, their ability, their behavior, their communities, or their family that will harm their confidence or their relationships with educators and school leaders.

Second, this tactic helps to shape the communication among educators and school leaders by reminding them of the impact and implications of their words. If school leaders and educators want to create a school culture in which failure is not seen as a default for any child, they should start with displaying empathy in their communication.

Speaking negatively about students, their families, and their communities can also impact an educator's or school leader's personal attitudes and those of their colleagues. Pinpointing student and community shortcomings and deficits without recognizing strengths, expressing futility or the impossibility of reaching individuals or groups of students, and venting excessively about the personal and behavioral characteristics of students reinforces educators' feelings of lack of teacher efficacy.

Provide families with all the relevant information about their children. Educators and school leaders should systematically provide families with all the information they need about their children's education. This should include grade and assessment information as well as both positive and negative information about student performance, achievement, and behavior in school. Educators and school leaders should specifically provide information and discuss any assessments that will be used to make decisions that will impact students in the moderate and/or long term.

Educators and school leaders should plan to give families the information they will need to effectively take part in decision making and to effectively advocate for their children. This should include information about how decisions are made in the school or system and how current decisions are likely to impact future educational decisions for their children. This information should be provided in the family's home language.

Eradicate vocabulary that communicates limitations to student abilities. For educators and school leaders, shaping one's communication and carefully choosing one's vocabulary is much more than simply attempting to be politically correct. Because effective teaching and learning rely on positive, meaningful relationships, trust, and daily interaction, educators and school leaders must be careful to communicate caring and respect in every situation. Additionally, the words that educators and school leaders use send messages to their colleagues about the acceptable beliefs and culture of the school and system.

Educators and school leaders should specifically identify the words and phrases used in their schools that send a message of otherness, dehumanization, and negative attitudes toward individuals or groups of students. They should then discuss the meaning of these words and the messages they may send about or to students and families. School leaders and educators should agree to eliminate these words from their vocabularies and use student-first language that communicates the value of every student.

Chapter Seven

Attitudes and Beliefs

In eleventh-grade history class, I sparred with my favorite and most frustrating teacher about the way in which students were selected for the honors program. Mr. McKenzie explained that the students in honors classes were the "cream of the crop." They were the students whose test scores placed them at the top of their class as incoming freshmen. As a result, they deserved to be in classes where they would not have to interact with or be held back by lesser students.

Students in the honors classes were given activities to prepare for the ACT test because, as Mr. McKenzie explained, they were the college-bound students. Students in the other levels of classes were not given this advantage because they were likely to go into the military or get a job right out of high school. There was no need to waste time preparing them for a college entrance exam. When I protested, Mr. McKenzie said simply, "That's just the way it is."

One day, I spoke to Mr. McKenzie about another student whose request to enter an honors class was denied. I explained that the student was a hard worker who had earned straight As in all his regular-level courses. Surely, a student like this could succeed in an honors-level course. Mr. McKenzie responded by saying that regardless of the student's hard work, he simply was not "honors material."

Educators' attitudes and beliefs about their students matter. As human beings, all educators and leaders have beliefs, attitudes, and biases that impact the way they view their students and the communities they serve. The development of biases that affect instruction and decision making is unavoidable. For that reason, it is imperative that educators and school leaders examine their attitudes and beliefs and cultivate actions that support student learning.

Of all the components of failure as a default, attitudes and beliefs are, by far, the most difficult to effectively change. However, they are particularly important because they influence the decisions made in every other area. Educators can, and should, change the structures and messages that perpetuate the achievement gap. Educators and leaders must also cultivate attitudes and beliefs that will contribute to success. Without a change of beliefs, decision makers will continue to make decisions that are grounded in failure as a default anytime they are not specifically led to plan for student success.

This phenomenon is evident in schools that make rapid improvements under the strong leadership and clear structures of one school administrator only to return to previous ways of doing things when that leader leaves. Similarly, this phenomenon is seen when schools implement highly structured programs, such as those required under Reading First, Race to the Top, and School Improvement Grants.

In each of these programs, a significant portion of the grant resources are devoted to professional development and training for educators to build capacity and make the new structures and strategies part of the culture of the schools where they are implemented. However, only when a predominant number of staff members adopt a new set of attitudes and beliefs (and those staff members remain on the staff) do the changes last.

The educator attitudes and beliefs that most definitively impact the achievement gap are those that focus on a student's identity, value, and ability. The central, unspoken questions are: Who is this student? Is this child worth it? What can this student do? Educators' beliefs about these questions not only impact the decisions they make in schools, but they also affect educator interactions with students and their families and, in turn, students' beliefs about themselves and the schools they attend.

IDENTITY

The question of identity is of critical importance to children, as a key aspect of child development is the development of cultural, family, and individual identity. Schooling has the potential to significantly impact each student's sense of identity. Educators' beliefs about the identities of their students not only include who the students are now but also their origins and who they will be in the future. Educators' beliefs about their students' identities consciously or unconsciously impact the decisions they make about instruction.

If either the educator or the student perceives that the child's identity is at odds with educational achievement and attainment, teaching and learning will be impacted accordingly. In addition, if an educator or school leader associates a student's identity with aggressiveness, disrespect, or criminality, the educator or leader will view the student as a threat, treat the student with distrust, and/or discipline the student more harshly. This is where America's history of racism, nationalism, and classism has the greatest negative impact on schooling.

Sometimes students and families have internalized the idea that high achievement is not for them. Examples of this would be when parents say, "He's just not good at math. Neither was I," "People from this neighborhood don't go to college," "Middle school graduation may be the only graduation our kids will ever have," or "These boys just don't like school."

The effect of historical biases is also evident among students in some schools. Although much debated when labeled as "oppositional culture" by John Ogbu, the tendency still exists in some schools to identify high achievement and compliance with the characteristics of whiteness. Even when students do not label certain behaviors as "acting white," as was the case in Ogbu's studies, they, like their teachers, sometimes believe high-level educational programs are not for them (Fordham and Ogbu 1986).

This belief is strengthened by the underrepresentation of low-income students, African American students, and Latino students in gifted, honors, Advanced Placement, International Baccalaureate, and other specialized academic programs. It is also shored up by the overrepresentation of the same groups of students in special education, remedial programs, and school discipline. Students quickly recognize when students like them make up the bulk of programs for students who struggle and only a small percentage of programs for students who excel.

Educators and school leaders most frequently fall into this trap by making or embracing negative predictions about who and what students will become. These predictions may be based on who the students' parents are, where the students live, how the students look or dress, the school involvement of their families, or how the students behave. Alternatively, educators and school leaders may tie predictions to schooling-related factors, such as the students' labels, grades, reputations with past educators, test scores, perceived intelligence, or the past performance of students like them.

Whatever the reasoning behind negative predictions about student out-comes, such predictions have an adverse impact on every decision made about or for students as well as the level of effort given by both educators and students.

VALUE

Closely aligned with educator and school leader beliefs about student identity are their beliefs about their students' relative value and place in the community and society. The concept of a student's value ties directly to the level of efficacy and urgency educators and school leaders feel about producing high achievement. When educators and school leaders believe they are educating future leaders and individuals of high status, they demonstrate this belief through their plans for and interactions with the students and their parents.

On the other hand, when school leaders and educators believe their students are unlikely to escape poverty, achieve high status, or make significant contributions to the community or society, they seldom demonstrate a sense of efficacy or urgency to promote high achievement. Instead, educators and school leaders with these beliefs lament the circumstances and characteristics of "these kids."

Notably, most schools in the United States serve student populations that include both students who are believed to be of high status and value and students who are believed to be of low status and value. In these settings, the sense that students have different relative values can be palpable by students, educators, school leaders, and outside observers.

ABILITY

Ability is an important yet elusive concept in schools. For many educators, a student's ability is equated with his or her IQ. Many schools do both achievement and ability testing to make decisions about students. However, even in the absence of ability testing data, the idea of intelligence is such a popular concept that educators and leaders often believe they can determine a student's ability level based on observation or predict his or her intelligence based on demographics. Once educators and school leaders believe they know a student's ability, they make decisions and interact with the student accordingly.

The beliefs that may be the most detrimental to the achievement of African American students, Latino students, and low-income students are that educators can determine a student's ability or intelligence level, that a student's intelligence as measured by ability and IQ tests determines his or her success in society, that a student's ability and intelligence level is fixed and immutable, and that intelligence is linked to race, ethnicity, and income. Unfortunately, these false beliefs are seldom discussed or challenged in schools, and most educators receive little or no instruction in educational psychology or psychometry.

SOURCES OF FAILURE AS A DEFAULT BELIEF SYSTEM

Attitudes and beliefs that contribute to failure as a default can be the result of bias, prejudice, and stereotypes developed by an individual, a group, or society as a whole. Alternatively, these attitudes and beliefs can be the result of misunderstandings about human growth and development, misconceptions about teaching and learning, or overgeneralizations of conclusions drawn from prior experiences. Rarely are the attitudes and beliefs the result of overt racial, ethnic, or class hatred. Attitudes and beliefs that come from different sources are addressed through different strategies.

Bias, Prejudice, and Stereotypes

The history of racial, ethnic, and class discrimination in the United States has left our society with a long list of stereotypes, biases, and prejudicial beliefs. Many of these are disguised as ideas about racial, class, or cultural differences. The biases that are prevalent in society cannot help but infect schools. Societal biases are strengthened by racial and cultural segregation and isolation. Unfortunately, community segregation and racial and cultural isolation are typically reflected in schools.

When educators and school leaders come to school with stereotypes, biases, and prejudicial beliefs, it is important that those beliefs be examined and challenged. Simply silencing prejudicial beliefs and banishing them from polite conversation does not eliminate their impact on students in the school. Instead, colleagues and leaders must confront racism, classism, nationalism, and other forms of bias and actively teach human diversity and equity.

If educator and school leader bias stems from a lack of knowledge of and experience with people and communities with different backgrounds, and educators and school leaders are willing to engage in learning to understand diverse experiences and viewpoints, then eradicating bias can be achieved through an educational process. Breaking down stereotypes, biases, and prejudicial beliefs involves a process of frequent interaction, purposeful reflection, and meaningful discussion with those who are considered to be the "other."

Individuals going through this process must develop a sense of empathy that will allow them to identify with the experiences and viewpoints of people who are different from them.

Sadly, not all bias is the result of a lack of knowledge and experience. When educators and school leaders possess hardened stereotypes and long-held biases and prejudicial beliefs that they feel they must maintain and defend, there is little that others can do to change their beliefs. In these cases, the only way for school and system leaders to eradicate the bias from a school is to usher such individuals out of the school.

Otherwise, the students against whom the individual is biased will suffer, and the virus of prejudice will be passed to students.

Misunderstandings about Growth and Development

Another source of attitudes and beliefs that contribute to failure as a default is a misunderstanding of growth and development. The most common misunderstanding about growth and development is that human growth and development are or should be culture-free and, therefore, should be the same regardless of a person's background and experiences. They are not. Human development is strongly impacted by culture, resulting in different expectations for growth and development from families and communities of different backgrounds.

Because many educators believe growth and development are culture-free, they base their understanding about students on their own view or recollection of normal growth and development. When student development varies from what they perceive as normal, educators tend to attribute the cause of deviations from the perceived norm to deficits within the students. Even when students perform better in other areas, this is not seen as making up for the perceived deficit.

It is common to associate differences in growth and development with differences in ability. As a result, children from low-income families, Latino children, and African American children whose ways of life are different from white middle class children are frequently thought to have lower ability or to be developmentally delayed in some way. It is important that educators and school leaders learn about human diversity and the impact of culture on child development.

Misconceptions about Teaching and Learning

Another contributor to failure as a default is misconceptions about teaching and learning. Such misconceptions abound, particularly among educators and school leaders with limited experience and exposure and among those who have not continued to build their expertise through ongoing education, research, and study.

A prevalent misconception about teaching and learning is that learning is or should be automatic for children of average intelligence. This misconception is often applied to the development of reading skills, but it also may be applied to math and other areas. When educators believe learning should be automatic, they are less likely to plan strategically for student learning. They are also more likely to view any difficulty with quickly learning new skills as an indicator of low intelligence.

While children may learn some skills rapidly and without what seems to be much effort, it is to be expected that not all skills will come so easily. This is not an indicator of low intelligence. Instead, it is an indication that the student needs high-quality instruction to acquire the new skills.

Other frequent misconceptions about teaching and learning include the idea that the answer to learning difficulties lies in drills and repetition, that difficulty at the start of learning a concept or skill indicates a lack of ability to develop that skill well in the long term, that high-level critical-thinking skills can be taught through low-level activities, that there is such a thing as homogeneous grouping and that teaching can be made easier if teachers can group the same kinds of students together, and that specific teaching methods are what is termed as "just good teaching."

All these misconceptions reflect a lack of pedagogical knowledge that has a detrimental impact on the learning of students who struggle. African American students, Latino students, and low-income students are most frequently subjected to attempts to promote learning by grouping students together for low-level activities, drills, and repetition.

When this does not result in the development of high-level critical-thinking skills, educators and school leaders may assume that students cannot develop these skills. So they continue to provide more and more low-level activities, thereby creating a vicious cycle.

Unarticulated Societal Beliefs Regarding Public Education

Some attitudes and beliefs that support failure as a default are the result of the failure of society to clarify, embrace, and promote societal beliefs about public education that are necessary to promoting the educational success of all children. In the absence of these societal beliefs, individuals enter the field of education without a commitment to meeting the needs of all students.

A central, but little discussed, tenet of public schooling is the idea of "zero reject." Zero reject is the concept that public schools are to accept and educate all children regardless of who they are, where they are from, what their abilities are, how they look, how much money their parents have, or how they behave. Educators are to teach every child who comes through the door.

When educators embrace an attitude of zero reject, this belief influences all the decisions they make. But all too often, this central tenet of public education is never discussed among those who are responsible for educating children. So in practice, schools and school systems are structured to reject and exclude students who are too far from the ideal. This happens when educators and school leaders excessively suspend students, expel students, segregate students, or counsel or allow students to drop out.

Another central tenet of public education is the often-stated belief that all children can learn and that they all should receive a quality education regardless of their background or zip code. This societal belief has been articulated frequently (often by politicians). However, our society has failed to operationalize this belief. As a result, the structures of education funding and resource allocation contradict this belief.

Because schools are largely funded by property taxes, school resources are significantly impacted by the zip codes and neighborhoods in which children live. Despite the frequent articulation of the belief that this should not be the case, the nation has not shown the political will necessary to change this funding and resource allocation structure.

CHANGING THE CULTURE OF BELIEF

Because attitudes and beliefs are so difficult to change, the educational leader's first line of defense when it comes to attitudes and beliefs is exclusively bringing people into the organization whose attitudes and beliefs support student success. This demands that leaders plan a candidate screening process that includes gathering information about candidates' attitudes and beliefs as well as their experiences and training.

Leaders who are looking for staff members who will help to close the achievement gap must first make a clear distinction between those who are willing to teach and lead in the community and those who are wanting to teach and lead in the community. It is not uncommon in the teacher search process to find educators who are willing to work with a particular population of students.

They may be willing to do so because they need to secure a position, because the position pays better than others, or because they love the job of teaching enough to overlook the population of students with whom they would work. They may also be willing to devote a few years of service out of a sense of charity or obligation.

Teachers who are willing to serve a school's population of students are very different than teachers who want to serve that population. It is important to fill our schools with teachers who have an active and ongoing desire to work with the full diversity of students within the schools in which they teach. Like the willing teacher, the wanting teacher may have a sense of obligation to serve the students.

However, they are much more likely to see serving students in the school as a part of their core mission. This is critically important during the down times and difficult times that frequently occur in teaching and educational administration.

Educational leaders can search out candidates who desire to work in schools that serve students in poverty, African American students, and Latino students. There are many cases, however, in which educators have been assigned to schools serving the population they wanted to serve, but over time, the population of students and the makeup of the community changed around them. When this is the case, it can be very difficult for educators to adjust to their new reality. In these situations, educators are often faced with their own attitudes, beliefs, and biases that have never been examined.

At times, these educators also feel a sense of frustration because it feels like they have been the victim of a bait and switch. They started their educational career working with a particular group of students in a particular way, but over time, things have changed so significantly that they no longer recognize the profession they entered years ago.

When this is the case, it is important not to condemn educators for feeling this way or for expressing the unfairness of this experience. Doing so only serves to discourage educators from engaging in an examination of the way their attitudes and beliefs impact their decision making.

Instead of either avoiding the discussion or devoting too much valuable professional development and collaboration time to lamenting the population change, educators and leaders should focus on determining the current needs of students and duties of the profession and deciding whether they will choose the profession, the school, and the job given the current situation.

If the answer is no, educational leaders should assist educators in considering other career options that make use of their knowledge, skills, and experience without making them responsible for the education of children they do not want to teach.

For educators and school leaders who enter and remain in the school setting, it is important to create a school environment that nurtures attitudes and beliefs that support student learning and success. It is not enough to simply hope that the caring nature of educators and school leaders will result in the eradication of attitudes and beliefs that contribute to failure as a default. School leaders and educators should take the following steps to address attitudes and beliefs in their schools.

Directly examine and, if necessary, confront attitudes and beliefs. School leaders must recognize the power of attitudes and beliefs to impact students in schools. If educators, school leaders, staff members, or students voice or demonstrate attitudes and beliefs that contribute to failure as a default, their colleagues, leaders, or teachers must confront and question those beliefs. If no one in the school calls such beliefs into question, their silence sends the message that those attitudes and beliefs are shared and accepted.

School leaders or educators who confront negative beliefs will only very rarely change an individual's beliefs. However, by challenging the negative belief, they may set the tone for the school, make others feel safe in their advocacy for children, and cause the person with the negative attitudes and beliefs to begin to examine his or her own biases.

Define and explicitly communicate the desired organizational attitudes and beliefs. The collective beliefs of the school community must be clearly articulated and discussed on a frequent basis. Ideally, these beliefs are written as a coherent statement that goes along with the school's mission and vision. School leaders should engage those individuals who make up the school community in discussing, drafting, revising, and adopting the school's statement of beliefs. Their involvement in this process is critical because statements of belief should guide all decisions that are made at the district, school, and classroom levels.

Moreover, this statement of beliefs should guide the development of policies as well as the selection of staff members, educators, and school leaders. Before an educator or school leader signs on to work in a school, he or she should know and be able to commit to the school's statements of belief. These policies should not change simply due to the turnover of one or more staff members. Instead, the school community should periodically revisit, revise if necessary, and reaffirm its statement of beliefs.

Specifically eradicate language that reinforces attitudes and beliefs that failure is a default. The language used by adults in schools is a window whereby others can view the attitudes and beliefs that are prevalent in the school. In addition, as discussed in Chapter 6, language can help to perpetuate and spread specific attitudes and beliefs throughout the organization and community. Simply changing the language used in schools does not change the attitude and beliefs. However, changing the language can change the likelihood of negative attitudes and beliefs being promoted. In addition, when adults in schools use language that reflects the school's statement of belief, those collective beliefs are strengthened.

Ask questions that force educators to think about the identity and value of their students. Assumptions about the identity, status, and value of students can often persist in the school environment. Because it is human nature to judge one another's identity, status, and value, school leaders and educators who want to eliminate failure as a default must bring these kinds of assumptions and judgments to light.

As educators and school leaders discuss curriculum and/or make decisions about instruction, interventions, and assessments, they should ask themselves and one another to describe the future for which they are preparing their students. What options do they want their students to have? To what extent do the decisions they are making prepare their students for short, moderate, and long-term success? What limitations are they inadvertently placing on their students' future choices? Would the decisions they are making for their students be good enough for the educators' and school leaders' own children?

Frequently review the evidence of student ability and the impact that educator practice has on student outcomes. School leaders and educators must continuously combat a lack of teacher efficacy. When school leaders have negative attitudes and beliefs about the ability of their students to succeed, their sense of efficacy suffers because they believe that their practice will have little or no impact on student achievement.

This feeling is often exacerbated by accountability tests and other assessments that provide test scores with little other information that can be used for learning about students or planning curriculum and instruction. In situations in which students take a test that is then collected and shipped away for scoring, educators and school leaders can begin to feel as though the work they do is completely disconnected from student achievement. As a result, educators and school leaders take neither the blame for low test scores nor the credit for high ones.

School leaders must assist educators and colleagues to make a clear connection between the quality of their practice and the outcomes for students. This can be done using local assessments that are developed, administered, and scored by the educators within the school. It also can be done by conducting action research and reviewing and analyzing the qualitative and quantitative results of specific instructional practices on student achievement. Most of all, it is imperative that educators and school leaders engage in these discussions so they can develop a meaningful picture of their students' ability to learn and their ability to affect student learning.

Train educators to implement best practices that produce positive outcomes. Discuss the relationship between educator best practices and student success. Educators and school leaders should continuously combat the ideas that best practices are "just good teaching" and that student success is a function of the student's intelligence, effort, or motivation alone.

Good teaching involves the ability and willingness to develop a broad repertoire of skills, strategies, and methods to teach students (with diverse needs and ways of engaging and learning) in ways that will allow them to learn. Each of those skills, methods, and strategies has specific steps that good teachers must learn to implement strategically.

When educators and school leaders select from their pedagogy and leadership toolboxes the strategies and methods students need, students at all levels of intelligence, effort, and motivation can learn and succeed at a higher level than they would be able to achieve alone. This is the power of teaching and leadership.

Discuss educator candidates' specific reasons for wanting to work in your school and with your students. To the greatest extent possible in their communities, school leaders should be very selective when seeking teachers, school leaders, and staff for their schools. There are many noble, meaningful, and fulfilling professions other than being an educator or school leader. School and district leaders should work diligently to ensure that they hire only individuals who have the skills, talent, and desire to work in their specific setting and with their specific children.

If the best available candidate is missing a certain skill or set of skills, school leaders can provide training and support to help the individual build her or his skills. On the other hand, school leaders cannot provide any kind of training that will create a talent for teaching where it does not exist. Nor can school leaders attempt to change the desires of candidates who do not specifically want to work with low-income students, Latino students, or African American students.

If the candidate seems to be making a sacrifice by agreeing to work with the full range of students in a school, that candidate would likely be more successful somewhere else.

Prior to making a hiring decision, school leaders should share their school and district's belief statement with the preferred candidate. They should ask the candidate to talk about each of the beliefs identified in the belief statement. If the candidate is unable to articulate his or her own beliefs or if the candidate is unable to support the beliefs, the candidate would likely fit in better in another school or district.

Provide all current and preservice educators and school leaders with training on child development, including language development and human diversity. Training on human development and in-depth training in pedagogy are conspicuously missing from some teacher education programs and most in-service professional development. To effectively support learning and success for the diverse population of students in schools, educators and school leaders must develop a high level of expertise in understanding student growth and development as well as the methods that will most effectively promote learning.

This level of expertise cannot be accomplished with a four- or five-year teacher preparation program. It must be acquired through both preservice training and ongoing in-service professional development and study with different students and in different settings.

Chapter Eight

For Policy Makers

"If we decline to invest in the children of immigrants, just because they don't look like us, we diminish the prospects of our own children—because those brown kids will represent a larger share of America's workforce. And our economy doesn't have to be a zero-sum game."

—Barack H. Obama (2017)

It is important to never underestimate the power of policy to shape the quality of education children receive. Just like educators and school leaders, well-meaning policy makers; legislators; and community, state, and national leaders can inadvertently make decisions, send messages, and establish structures that contribute to the achievement gap.

Perhaps the most important, and yet the most difficult, thing for educational policy makers to understand and accept is that their positive intentions, policy research, and best-laid plans for improving schools for African American students, Latino students, and low-income students are easily negated by failure as a default. The many negative impacts of the school-accountability and school-reform movement stem in large part from the implementation of educational laws and policies that were created to benefit students.

When educators, leaders, and community members operate under a collective belief that failure is a default for some children, no carefully planned policies, regulations, or procedures can overcome the power of the structures, messages, and attitudes upon which schooling is built. This creates a true dilemma for educational policy makers who desire to close the achievement gap. Punishing educators and leaders, testing students more, shaming schools that do not achieve required results, and closing or restructuring schools do not change the underlying cause for the persistent achievement gap in schools.

At times, when policy makers create rules and laws to legislate excellent teacher performance and student achievement, the same legislation that moves some to action builds obstacles for others. The question, then, for policy makers is how to encourage, assist, and empower schools to eradicate the belief that failure is a default for some students without creating conditions that contribute to the perpetuation of the gap.

WHAT EDUCATIONAL POLICY CAN (AND CANNOT) DO

The significance of educational policy is undeniable. One need simply consider the impact of No Child Left Behind and the larger school accountability movement to note how federal and state policies impact schools. Indeed, one of the recurring criticisms of these laws is that they have negatively influenced public school curricula, recruitment and retention of teachers, and community involvement in schools.

It is important, however, for policy makers to recognize the difference between what educational policies can and cannot do. Most significantly, when it comes to raising student achievement and closing the achievement gap, policy makers cannot write a law or establish a set of rules that will change widespread beliefs. In addition, educational policies cannot directly legislate student achievement and attainment outcomes nor can they negate the effects of generations of failure as a default.

When designing new policies, policy makers must understand and plan for the diffuse nature of America's public school system. Each new law and policy is distributed through fifty states, thousands of school districts, tens of thousands of schools, and hundreds of thousands of classrooms. At each level of distribution, opportunities for diversion from the policy's initial intent exist. Educators and leaders interpret and operationalize laws and policies based on their own beliefs, circumstances, and experiences.

In the end, policy makers have the power, through legislation, policies, rules, and guidance, to influence the decisions and priorities of educators and leaders. They must use this power wisely because their influence is limited to structures that can be built and messages that can be sent. The power and influence of policy makers does not extend to dictating attitudes, eliminating biases, or single-handedly eliminating failure as a default.

To combat the achievement gap and end failure as a default in our schools, policy makers must focus on the things that education policy can do effectively in the school systems we have today. This includes supporting and guiding educators, leaders, and communities in ways that are meaningful, effective, and sustainable. Education policy should empower, encourage, and drive educators and leaders who are serving the best interests of all students. It should make ignoring the needs of children difficult in any setting.

Education policy makers can proactively address some of the recurring areas of dispute in education policy. These include the educator's role in education policy development, the impact of noneducation public policy on the achievement gap, the focus on equity or excellence, and the influence of money on education.

The Educator's Role in Education Policy

Effective policy makers must rely on educators and leaders, working with their communities, to eradicate failure as a default and provide the highest-quality of education to all children. Since changing the day-to-day experiential curriculum that African American children, Latino children, and low-income children receive in schools is largely dependent on educators and leaders, it is vital that policy makers learn to support, empower, guide, and be guided by educators and leaders to improve and enhance education for all of America's children. An often-decried aspect of state and federal education policy is the fact that it is typically created by individuals with little or no experience as educators or school leaders. Frontline educators and leaders seldom play a significant role in shaping education policy. The result is that policies are written without the benefit of the experiences of those who have dedicated their lives to public education. Therefore, educators and school leaders become victims who must simply react to policy changes.

Education laws and policies are typically developed at the state or federal level. Once the proposed laws or rules are released, educators and leaders who are in tune with the process provide feedback and comment to try to influence the final format of the policy. This after-the-fact input results in policies that often do not go as far as policy makers intended but go beyond what educators and leaders believe is right. Through this process, education policy becomes a hodgepodge of different rules that weaken the system and poorly address the issues for which they were created.

Policy makers at all levels should involve educators and leaders with current firsthand experience serving children and leading public schools throughout the policy development process. First, educators and school leaders should be engaged to help fully define the problems to be addressed by a policy. Then, they should be allowed to brainstorm the specific, realistic consequences of implementing the proposed policy, including the ways in which educators and leaders in different situations are likely to operationalize the policy.

Educators and school leaders are most able to guide policy makers on providing the support necessary to ensure that policies are implemented effectively. School leaders and educators can also provide consultation about other policies that potentially impact schools.

Noneducation Public Policy and the Achievement Gap

Perhaps more than any other area, public education is powerfully impacted by public policy in many other areas. National, state, and community issues, from the complex and controversial to the simple and mundane, influence the experiential curriculum students receive in schools.

In 2016, when the state of Illinois finally decided, after months of mounting bills, to fund pre-K through twelfth-grade schools for the entire year, they neglected to fund childcare, mental health services, home health care, and numerous other services for low-income and disabled families (Garcia, Geiger, and Dardick 2016). They also conspicuously left out higher education. Children were able to go to school, but their learning was negatively impacted by the loss of services for them and their families. Schools were not equipped or funded to make up the slack for poor public policy.

Similarly, try as they might, educators cannot erase the impact of crime and gun violence in the community, eliminate mental health issues in families, or ensure prenatal and child preventive care and health care. Yet all these things, and myriad others, impact the experiential curriculum and access to education and, therefore, the quality of education that children receive. Every policy that addresses these kinds of issues should be treated like an education policy.

If education policy makers have a serious commitment to closing the achievement gap and ensuring a high quality of education for all children, they must improve all aspects of public policy that impact children and families, particularly those who are low income or English-language learning or impacted by mental illness, violence, substance abuse, health issues, disabilities, or incarceration. Similar to education policy, educators and school leaders should have a meaningful role in the development and implementation of public policy affecting children and families.

Equity versus Excellence

The question of when public education should be focused on equity or excellence is often a proxy battle between those who desire to raise the education ceiling by focusing efforts on high-achieving students and those seeking to raise the floor by placing an emphasis on improving the performance of students and schools that struggle. As the school-reform-and-accountability movement has progressed, educational policy has vacillated between a focus on equity and a focus on excellence. However, at this point in education history, the foci of equity and excellence must converge.

The diversity of families and children in the United States is such that a lack of emphasis on equity results in the continual decline of overall educational achievement, attainment, and competitiveness of students in the United States. One of the reasons that student achievement, as measured by national and international standardized tests, has not improved significantly for the past twenty years is the increasing diversity of America's students.

If low-income children, African American children, and Latino children routinely receive a lower quality of education in America schools, and if the percentage of students in those groups increases year after year, it is easy to see why overall achievement stagnates or declines when compared to other nations'.

In America's diverse public school system, equity versus excellence is a false dichotomy, arguments about which will not result in the outcomes policy makers and citizens desire from schools. The only way to achieve the kinds of outcomes that are necessary to regain and maintain our competitive edge is to provide a system in which every child, family, and community can depend on both excellence and equity in their school. In short, there is no excellence in our system without equity.

A Word about Money in Education

A key aspect of educational equity involves education funding. Educators, researchers, and policy makers frequently debate the importance of money in improving student achievement and closing the achievement gap. Some researchers and policy makers argue that increases in education spending over the years have not produced commensurate increases in test scores. What they do not realize is that money itself does not impact student achievement test scores. Instead, the amount of financial resources available to families, schools, and communities is related to the quality of education students receive.

The provision of funds directly impacts the programs and structures that students experience in schools. In addition, the amount of funds provided, the ways in which funds are allocated, the priorities of the use of funds, and the relative availability of discretionary funds reveal attitudes and beliefs and communicate messages as powerfully as anything else we do in schools. The most frequent reason for inequity in school resources, exposure, and experiences is a lack of funding in schools and districts that serve low-income communities (many of which serve high percentages of African American and Latino students).

In one school district, students never learn to swim because their schools do not have pools. In another school district, students have a natatorium,[1] in which they learn to swim, swim competitively, and play water polo. In one school district, students visit the school library multiple times per week to check out books to read independently. In another school district, there is no school or community library available, and students are not allowed to bring their schoolbooks home because they may lose them. No amount of educator training, accountability measures, or learning standards can compensate for these differences in school resources and student experiences.

As a practical matter, money is needed to provide all students with the inputs that should be common for all students. Schools without the local resources to provide the necessary inputs need additional funds to provide the resources and experiences students need. Schools that provide sufficient educational inputs can do so in large part because of the financial resources of their school systems, families, and communities.

A frequent way to address funding inequities is the practice of establishing a foundational level of funding that should be available to serve students. It is argued that equity is improved by ensuring a minimal level of funding for the education of students. One problem with this approach is determining the minimal level of funding that is adequate. Because there has been no agreement about the educational inputs that are necessary for all students, the foundational level of funding provided to schools is seldom adequate in schools without supplemental resources.

Providing all schools with a foundational level of funding does not mitigate educational inequity. Students in schools in middle class and wealthy school districts benefit from the extensive supplemental resources of their families and communities. Students in low-income school districts do not.

COMBATING THE ACHIEVEMENT GAP

The most effective educational policies for closing the achievement gap that can be implemented at the federal and state level will include creating and promoting collective statements of belief, establishing and supporting standards of input, developing meaningful measures of inputs and outcomes, and addressing the failure as a default cycle.

Create Collective Statements of Belief

The beliefs espoused by educators, leaders, and policy makers are incredibly important in shaping the structures and messages of schools. The power of creating collective statements of belief does not lie in forcing people to change their long-standing beliefs. Rather, the power of this process lies in exposing and exploring the beliefs upon which the system is built. In addition, clear statements of belief, when adhered to, have a significant impact on the selection of individuals who choose the education field in specific schools and the education field in general.

The success of public education at ensuring a high-quality education to all children requires that educators, leaders, and policy makers embrace fundamental beliefs about schooling. One belief that has been fundamental to public schools that serve all students is the idea of "zero reject." Public schools must serve all children regardless of their backgrounds, family income, predicted ability, disability, level of motivation, etc. Zero reject is the most significant difference between public schools and private, charter, and independent schools.

Other beliefs that are fundamental to the creation of equitable and excellent public schools include the belief that public education serves a public purpose that makes it worth the investment in schools; the conviction that all children can learn and that the level of learning a child can achieve is something neither educators nor others can predict; and the belief that all children have a right to and deserve to learn and succeed at the highest possible level regardless of the merit (or lack thereof) of their communities, families, or identities. These beliefs represent core beliefs of public education.

These beliefs, supplemented by the collective beliefs of the school and community, should be articulated clearly and often. They should guide policy development and decision making. Well-articulated collective guiding beliefs aid in the setting of priorities for the use of financial and human resources, the design and implementation of curriculum and instruction, and the process of educator and school leader recruitment and retention.

It is key that beliefs related to public education be articulated and shared collectively. In the absence of well-articulated collective beliefs, decision making will be guided by numerous disparate beliefs, many of which may not be compatible with the creation of equitable and excellent public schools. Policy makers can combat the achievement gap by promoting the development and articulation of collective statements of belief to guide decision making in and about schools.

Support Standards of Input

Experience and exposure matter. Teaching and leadership matter. Resources and expectations matter. As long as it is acceptable for students in different communities, different schools, or different households to receive dramatically different resources, expectations, and experiences in schools, the idea of equitable or excellent outcomes will continue to be a farce.

One of the most powerful things policy makers can do to combat the achievement gap is address the inequities students experience in schools by establishing standards of input, such as those described in Chapter 4. Standards of input can be used to establish common expectations for a quality education. By establishing common expectations of the resources and experiences all students deserve from schools, policy makers can guide decision making about the allocation and use of education funds and other resources.

The process of creating and supporting standards of input has been undertaken by professional organizations in the past. Groups such as the National Association for the Education of Young Children (NAEYC) have developed standards of input in the form of program accreditation or program quality standards. They have successfully influenced the quality of early childhood education programs in schools and other organizations that have pursued NAEYC accreditation as well as those that have simply used the standards as a guide for program development or improvement (www.naeyc.org).

Standards of input should not simply be used as another accountability measure, nor should they be used in a way that is like today's school report cards, in which a school's status of meeting the standards is simply used to inform parents so that those with the means and resources to do so can choose schools that meet the standards while others are left in schools that do not have the desired resources. Instead, standards of input should be used as both a description of what all students deserve from schools and a method to determine the resources and supports that should be provided to all schools.

To be effective, educational standards of input must be created in a way that takes into account the knowledge and views of a wide range of education professionals, school leaders, families, and community members from different communities and various backgrounds. Those charged with drafting the educational input standards should include urban, suburban, and rural communities from each region of the nation as well as individuals from different ethnic groups and social classes. They should be individuals with strong ties to public schools and should reflect the diversity and interests of the public school student population.

The guiding question for the entirety of the standards of input development process should be "What do all students need, want, and deserve from schools to have the greatest chance of success in our society?" Throughout the process, participants should ask themselves, "Given the opportunity, what would I demand from a school for my child?"

Those who are from high-income communities should think about the impact their school and community resources have on students' experiences. "What would be missing from the schooling of students in my community if specific resources were not available to them and families could not replace those experiences at home or in the community?"

Beyond creating the educational input standards, policy makers should support the implementation of those standards in all schools. Let it be clear that supporting standards of input for all schools means more than simply adopting standards, distributing them to school districts and schools across the nation, and punishing schools that do not meet them. The power of educational input standards is the recognition that all students from all backgrounds in all communities deserve access to specific kinds of resources.

To make the standards of input a reality, policy makers must work with states and school districts to ensure that all schools have the funding, human resources, and capacity to meet the standards of input. Without this key step, establishing educational input standards will only spotlight the unsustainable inequity of the school system.

Steps to supporting standards of input will include engaging educators and school leaders in devising the best ways to provide professional development and build capacity among their peers; building widespread community and political support for the standards; examining the current inequities, including identifying schools and communities that currently do not have the resources or access identified by the standards; engaging directly with school and school system leaders to plan for and support improvement; engaging with teacher and school leader preparation programs to involve future generations of educators and school leaders; and providing grant funds and other funding flexibility necessary to ensure that resources can be provided.

Develop Meaningful Measures for Inputs and Outcomes

Excessive testing, penalties for poor performance, and failure as a default have led educators and leaders to narrow the curriculum, focus on test preparation, and make other decisions that work against the long-term interests of children. By establishing expected outcomes without addressing the inequities in inputs, laws, and policies, such as the No Child Left Behind Act, have made the prospect of closing the achievement gap seem laughable. All of this has led to a nationwide backlash against high-stakes testing as the method of holding schools accountable for outcomes.

The negative impacts of high-stakes testing and the subsequent backlash against using testing as an accountability measure are, in some ways, very unfortunate. For educators and leaders, assessment, sometimes in the form of testing, is an important element of teaching and learning. When used appropriately, assessments are powerful tools to monitor student learning, guide instruction, and inform the development and implementation of curriculum.

These tools are necessary to understand and meet the needs of all children in schools. Yet because of the ineffective use of testing in school accountability, much of the current generation of educators and leaders have experienced testing only in its most ineffective and least informative form.

As a result of the widespread use of high-stakes testing and the belief that failure is a default, many schools, districts, and states have made widespread and long-term decisions based on one or two testing sessions. In addition, because the scores have been seen as the highest priority, classroom, school, and district tests that previously had been used to monitor student learning and grade students have been eliminated and replaced with tests that are selected for their predictive value for high-stakes accountability tests.

Tests that are selected for their ability to predict how well a student will do on high-stakes standardized achievement tests are used quite differently than classroom and other tests selected to monitor student learning and inform instruction. Educators and leaders routinely use the results of predictive tests to group students, determine test prep activities, identify which students to prioritize for intervention, and target instruction on the specific skills needed to improve the percentage of students predicted to pass the high-stakes test.

The overall result of this process is that curriculum and instruction moves further and further away from the core learning standards and closer and closer to a narrowly targeted test preparation course. In addition, students in schools that narrowly target test preparation soon receive the very clear message that the test scores they achieve are their most important attribute.

In this situation, students spend hours practicing answering specific types of test questions and taking practice tests. In some schools, they see hallway displays of student test scores color coded (red, yellow, green, blue) based on proficiency level. In some schools, they take preliminary tests that predict the likelihood that they will pass the real test at the end of the year. They know that failing the test will result in their being "held back" or failing to graduate. These kinds of experiences are seldom commonplace in schools serving middle and upper class communities.

Because assessment is an important part of the teaching and learning process, policy makers should promote and support assessment policies that restore assessment to its rightful place in classrooms, schools, and districts. This includes providing information about individual students, past and current instruction, curriculum, and groups.

Effective assessment allows educators and school leaders to answer the following questions: What knowledge and skills do students possess and to what level? What gaps exist in student learning? What student misconceptions exist? Which students have fully developed a particular skill? To what extent can students demonstrate a particular skill in a novel situation? For what new learning experiences are students prepared?

By gaining the answers to these questions, educators and school leaders can determine the next steps in meeting the needs of all students. If gaps or misconceptions exist, educators can identify them and reteach. If students have fully developed a skill, educators can plan to extend student learning or use the mastered skill in future activities. By understanding how well a student can apply a skill in a novel situation, educators can determine whether the student has truly mastered the skill or needs more practice or experience.

It is natural for policy makers to choose to use assessment/testing as a tool for accountability. However, it is important to recognize that assessments designed for accountability and those designed to improve teaching and learning are two different things.

What is the appropriate use of assessment for accountability? Tests that are used for accountability should provide a broad snapshot of student performance based on common standards. Key to this idea is the word "snapshot" and the recognition that the tests are meaningful in an accountability context only when they are administered to many students consistently over multiple years. The validity of accountability tests is hindered when tests are modified frequently and/or used to make large-scale decisions about small groups of students. Using accountability tests to make decisions about individual students is the most detrimental policy for school accountability.

Broad-scale accountability tests used consistently with the same groups of students over several years can provide information about the quality of curriculum in schools and about the trajectory of student achievement in states, regions, and the nation as a whole. Under these circumstances, the information gleaned from tests can be meaningfully disaggregated to provide information about equity and the relative performance and needs of various groups.

When leaders and policy makers attempt to do this at a microlevel, applying it to individual school districts, schools, or classrooms, the data that is gleaned becomes highly unreliable. Data gathered in this way is not valid for making small-scale educational decisions.

There are, however, assessments that can be used for small-scale accountability. These assessments must be designed for this purpose and must tie directly to curriculum and instruction in the district, school, and classroom being assessed. These kinds of assessments can be used to compare the performance of students in a particular district, school, or classroom to a national or statewide criterion or norm. Unlike most state accountability tests, however, the standards upon which these tests are based are readily available to educators and school leaders and are linked to the district or school curriculum and day-to-day instruction.

Even in this situation, it is imperative for school leaders and policy makers to remember that accountability tests provide only a snapshot, which can be skewed for any number of reasons. It should never be used as the sole or main determinant of high-stakes decisions about individual students or individual teachers.

Instead, these snapshots can help provide guidance for school leaders and provide additional information for decision making along with other sources of information, such as student observations, teacher evaluations, program evaluations, and curriculum reviews. Taken together, these sources of information can appropriately be used to guide professional development, curricular selections, instructional changes, and student supports.

State and federal policy makers who would like to use accountability tests to make decisions at the district, school, or classroom level should consider a plan in which school leaders identify the combination of local assessments, curriculum and program evaluation data, and other information upon which to base goals and accountability. This approach can serve as the foundation of school improvement planning and local accountability.

Address the Failure as a Default Cycle

The failure as a default cycle is the confluence of a lack of urgency to eliminate the achievement gap created by a lack of teacher efficacy and supported by a lack of educator, leader, and institutional capacity to do what is necessary to meet the needs of all children. To address this cycle, policy makers must begin by addressing educator, leader, and institutional capacity.

Education is a people-intensive field in which the success of each school and classroom is dependent on the performance of multiple individuals. Building capacity, then, requires that resources, professional development, and support touch everyone. It also requires that professional learning be coherent and sustained and that educators and school leaders develop expertise beyond simple implementation of specific programs.

To support school capacity building, policy makers should recognize that teacher and school leader preparation programs are only the beginning of the development of outstanding educators and leaders. Teaching is a profession that requires the educator to possess broad and deep knowledge in many areas, including human development, psychology, sociology, curriculum, assessment, pedagogy, literacy development, language development, and all subject areas. Classroom diversity also requires that educators develop expertise in second language acquisition, disabilities, and all other specific needs that students may have.

Effective school and district administrators must possess all the same skills plus a deep understanding of leadership, group processes, adult learning, law, finance, community building, education policy, and politics. Even the most rigorous preparation programs produce novices who must continue to grow throughout their careers to meet the many challenges of educating all children.

Building capacity for educators means supporting continual educator study, training, reflection, and research throughout an educator's career. One way to do this is by ensuring that educators and school leaders have ready access to graduate school classes and continuing education courses. Many states have required a number of continuing education courses and/or professional development. Unfortunately, the quality, variety, and accessibility of these courses is impacted by the educator's or district's ability to pay. Moreover, the ability to recruit, hire, and retain teachers and school leaders who already possess experience, advanced training, and skills is often limited by a school's or district's ability to compete for such employees.

State and federal policy makers can strengthen educator capacity by working with colleges and universities and research institutions to provide tuition-free courses for educators and school leaders. Courses and programs can be offered in partnership with schools and districts to ensure local support. Similarly, undergraduate programs and alternative routes to teaching can be provided free of charge through scholarships for paraprofessionals and school volunteers with years of service and recommendations from school and district leaders.

Another option for policy makers is to promote national certification programs, such as the National Board for Professional Teaching Standards Certification. These programs provide educators with extensive additional training and engage educators in extensive reflection and self-assessment based on high standards. To achieve this level of certification, educators must submit a portfolio of documents, videos, and other evidence of their teaching skills and performance.

By promoting this kind of program, policy makers can help educators build and demonstrate their expertise. Nationally certified teachers contribute to the capacity of the schools and districts in which they work. Policy makers should consider offering programs that allow qualified educators to participate in a national certification program free of charge.

The most common way to build capacity in schools is by providing ongoing professional development at the school or district level. Job-embedded professional development is critical to increasing teacher capacity and effectiveness. Unfortunately, when funding is low or funding cuts are made, school- and district-level professional development is the first thing to go. Policy makers should support the provision of ongoing professional development to educators and school leaders in all schools by providing funds for professional development and/or providing schools with access to experts and professional developers in areas of need.

Next, policy makers must support teacher efficacy. For educators and school leaders to give full effort to closing the achievement gap, they must trust that their efforts will truly impact student outcomes. They must believe that their curricular choices and the quality of their instruction matter, and they must be able to see (qualitatively and quantitatively) the results.

Federal and state policy makers can best strengthen teacher efficacy by allowing and assisting educators and school leaders to monitor and track the progress of their current and past students. This should include a focus on cohorts of students so that educators can track and analyze student achievement, growth, and outcomes for the same group of students over time.

It is a mistake to limit the measurement of teacher impact to the measurement of test scores. When considering the efficacy of educator and school leader decisions, policy makers, school leaders, and educators should consider educators' impact on the lives of students. What has been the impact on students' educational attainment, college entry and completion, workforce participation, community citizenship and contribution, achievement of individual goals? These longer-term impacts are better indicators of the effectiveness of teacher and school leader decisions than the short-term snapshots provided by standardized tests.

In addition to quantitative methods of showing teacher efficacy, it is important for educators and school leaders to feel that their expertise, assessment, and qualitative analyses of student learning are meaningful and valid. This is part of treating educators and school leaders as professionals. Policy makers and school leaders should involve educators in analyzing the impacts of their decisions on students and using this information to develop their expertise and effectiveness.

As capacity and efficacy improve, policy makers can legitimately promote the urgency of closing the achievement gap. True urgency to improve student learning and achievement will not stem from new accountability laws or threats of punishment. As has been discussed, such attempts to create urgency lead to concern for student learning to be set aside in favor of desperation to avoid punishment and shame. True urgency to meet the needs of low-income students, Latino students, and African American students must be tied to educator and school leader beliefs about the value of their students and the standards of educational input that all students deserve.

Policy makers should promote the joint development of goals and timelines for improvement of student achievement for Latino students, African American students, and low-income students. Goals and timelines for improvement in student achievement must be jointly developed by school leaders, educators, and the communities they serve. They must be tied to well-articulated-and-funded educational input standards. They must be supported by specific action steps that are within the sphere of influence of educators and school leaders, and they must be realistic or they will be ignored by both educators and community members.

Perhaps the most important lesson for policy makers who are committed to combating the achievement gap despite the prevalence of failure as a default is that an understanding of failure as a default; a belief in the unlimited and unknowable potential of every child; a commitment to public education that meets high educational input standards for all children; and the meaningful involvement of educators, school leaders, and communities in planning for educational improvement must be integral to the process of developing and implementing effective education policy. Only together can educators, school leaders, families, and policy makers eradicate failure as a default and create a system that promotes short-, moderate-, and long-term success for every child.

NOTE

1. For those who, like me, have lived and worked in communities without such a thing, a "natatorium" is a separate building to house swimming pools.

Conclusion

Who Succeeds, Who Fails, Who Cares?

I recently took part in a discussion with other educators about the extreme differences in the experiences and roles of educators in different settings depending on the wealth and diversity of the community in which they work. Having worked in several school districts serving students with varying levels of poverty and a wide range of demographics, I have found that the day-to-day challenges of public education can vary widely between settings.

In some schools, there is a high level of parent and community support. This typically translates into having many parents and family members advocating vocally for their children's interests and routinely questioning the decisions of teachers, administrators, and board members. It also means the same parents and family members support and volunteer at the school and provide the students with many advantages in and outside of the school setting.

In other schools, parents and family members have little support and few resources to give to educators, school leaders, and students. In these schools, families follow the instructions of school staff in registering their children and making sure they attend school as required. They come to school when invited for special events and enforce with their children the expectation that they had "better not have to go up to the school" for their child's behavior. Beyond that, many families simply trust educators and school leaders to do right by their children by providing them with the education they need. Unfortunately, this is seldom enough.

In a society in which a quality education is treated as a scarce resource and failure is seen as the default for some children, children whose parents trust the system to work for their child often lose out on the quality education that they need. Unfortunately, even when African American families, Latino families, and low-income families have the resources to actively engage in school and advocate for their children, failure as a default makes acquiring a high-quality education difficult for these children.

To combat the achievement gap, educators and school leaders must do the work that families have entrusted to them. Educators and school leaders did not create failure as a default. Educators and school leaders of all backgrounds have been immersed in this ideology for many years. Educators, school leaders, and policy makers must have the awareness and moral courage to know better and do better for all children.

There are many outside factors that impact student achievement, the achievement gap, and the provision of quality public education. These include long-term policies and practices grounded in racism and classism as well as the impact of generational poverty. They include environmental injustices, such as children being routinely exposed to lead, students playing on school playgrounds built directly under power lines, and students living in houses built on toxic waste sites. They include food injustice, such as entire towns, cities, and large neighborhoods with no grocery store or other source of fresh fruits and vegetables, leaving children to get their breakfast, lunch, and dinner from fast-food restaurants and gas stations.

This book could address other factors such as unequal access to health care, including mental health and addiction care. It could include disparities in parental education levels and parenting practices. It could include exposure to violence, high levels of unemployment, lack of access to higher education and training, and myriad other factors that clearly and directly impact a student's success in school. The list of problems and injustices that educators, school leaders, families, and policy makers should engage in helping to address is long.

This book specifically and purposefully does not address the many causes of the achievement gap and failure as a default that lie outside of schools, school systems, and education policy. Although these causes are critically important to eliminating the achievement gap and achieving social justice, they lie firmly outside the daily spheres of influence of educators, school and system leaders, and educational policy makers. This book focuses specifically and exclusively on the role of educators, school leaders, and educational policy makers in eliminating failure as a default where they have the most power.

A foundational premise of this book is the idea of efficacy. Educators, school leaders, and educational policy makers must do what is within their power to raise student achievement and eliminate the achievement gap. This will make an untold difference in the experiences of children and families in school. Withholding efforts to eliminate failure as a default until the larger society corrects its problems with racism, classism, poverty, and social justice will only serve to deny additional generations of African American children, Latino children, and low-income children the quality of education that all children need and deserve.

Every year that large numbers of students fail to learn to read and develop the other skills, attitudes, and behaviors that they need to have success in our society is a tragedy that perpetuates the achievement gap. For every year that children of all races, backgrounds, and classes are taught through their experiential curriculum that failure can be expected for some individuals or groups because of who they are, failure as a default is extended for another generation. For every year that educators and school leaders without the capacity to serve all students believe that their efforts will never create success for some students, the failure as a default cycle starts anew.

Now is the time for each and every educator, school leader, and policy maker to confront and eliminate failure as a default in their practice, in their classroom, in their school, in their system, and in their community. They must all realize that no law, no test, and no accountability measures have the power that each individual and group of educators and leaders wield over the persistent achievement gap.

Private schools and charter schools cannot do it. Although they benefit some students, they leave other students behind in poorly resourced and markedly more segregated schools. In many settings, they exacerbate the inequities that already exist between and within schools.

Educators and school leaders create the experiential curriculum. By examining their practices and analyzing the signs and symptoms of failure as a default in the settings they shape, educators and school leaders can eradicate all indications of failure as a default from the structures, messages, attitudes, and beliefs in schools and systems all over the nation and world. What might happen if every low-income child, Latino child, and African American child attended schools in which they were immersed in a culture in which they were highly valued, expected to succeed, provided with expert instruction and support, and provided with every necessary resource?

What might happen if policy makers shaped educational policy to ensure that every child in every school had the resources they need along with educators and leaders who possess the capacity, teacher efficacy, and urgency to educate them to achieve success? What might happen if policy makers engaged with educators, school leaders, and families to plan to achieve these and related goals?

Who succeeds? Who fails? It all depends on who cares. If educators, school leaders, and policy makers care enough about combating the achievement gap to examine the attitudes, beliefs, messages, and structures that make up their practices and policies and to eliminate failure as a default, they can create a culture of success to benefit every child.

References

Allen, Janet. 1999. *Words, words, words: Teaching vocabulary in grades 4–12*. York, ME: Stenhouse Publishers.

American Library Association. American Library Association. www.ala.org (accessed March 28, 2016).

Barrington CUSD 220. Barrington Community Unit School District 220. www.barrington220.org (accessed: February 4, 2016).

Benjamin, Luddy T., Jr. 2009. The birth of American intelligence testing. *Monitor on Psychology* 40 (1): 20. apa.org/monitor/2009/01/assessment.aspx.

Blume, Howard. 2015. Achievement gaps widen for California's black and Latino students. *Los Angeles Times*, September 11. www.latimes.com/local/lanow/la-me-ln-achievement-gaps-widen-20150911-story.html.

Brown v. Board of Education, 347 U.S. 483 (1954) (USSC+).

Camera, Lauren. 2015. Study finds students underperform in schools with large black populations. *US News & World Report*, September 24. www.usnews.com/news/articles/2015/09/24/study-finds-students-underperform-in-schools-with-large-black-populations.

Camera, Lauren. January 13, 2016. Achievement gap between white and black students still gaping. *U.S. News & World Report*. January 13, 2016.

Camera, Lauren. March 28, 2016. Gains in reading for hispanic students overshadowed by achievement gaps. *U.S. News & World Report*. March 28, 2016.

Coleman, J. S. 1966. *Equality of educational opportunity study*. Washington, DC: US Department of Health, Education, and Welfare.

Default. *Dictionary.com Unabridged*. www.dictionary.com/browse/default, accessed February 4, 2016.

Douglass, Frederick. 1857. "West India Emancipation," speech delivered at Canandaigua, New York, August 4, 1857. In *The Life and Writings of Frederick Douglass*, edited by Philip S. Foner, vol. 2, p. 437 (1950).

Fletcher, Dan. 2009. Brief history: Standardized testing. *Time*. December 11. http://content.time.com/time/nation/article/0,8599,1947019,00.html.

Fordham, Signithia and John U. Ogbu. 1986. Black students' school success: Coping with the burden of "acting white." *Urban Review* 18 (3): 176–206.

Freire, P. 1972. *Pedagogy of the oppressed*. New York: Herder and Herder.

Garcia, Monique, Kim Geiger, and Hal Dardick. 2016. Rauner signs stopgap budget, school funding bill—but relief from stalemate proves temporary. *Chicago Tribune*, June 30. http://www.chicagotribune.com/news/local/politics/ct-illinois-budget-impasse-madigan-rauner-met-0701-20160630-story.html.

Glenwright, M. and P. M. Pexman. 2010, March. Development of children's ability to distinguish sarcasm and verbal irony. *Journal of Child Language* 37 (2): 429–51.

Graves, Joseph L., Jr. 2004. *The race myth: Why we pretend race exists in America.* New York: Penguin Group.

Hill, Teresa D. 2011. *Every closed eye ain't sleep: African American perspectives on the achievement gap.* Lanham, MD: Rowman & Littlefield Education.

H.R. 1804. 1994. 103rd Congress. Goals 2000: Educate America Act. https://www.govtrack.us/congress/bills/103/hr1804, accessed February 4, 2016.

Jefferson, Thomas. 1776. The Declaration of Independence. *Historic American Documents,* Lit2Go Edition. http://etc.usf.edu/lit2go/133/historic-american-documents/4957/the-declaration-of-independence/, accessed February 4, 2016.

Jordan, Winthrop D. 1969. Notes on the state of Virginia. In *The Negro Versus Equality.* Chicago: Rand McNally.

Kinney, T. April 29, 2016. Urban prep school in Chicago boasts 100 percent college acceptance rate, 7th year in a row. *Atlanta Black Star.* April 29, 2016.

Lott, Bernice. 2001. Low-income parents and the public schools. *Journal of Social Issues* 57 (2): 247–59. doi: 10.1111/0022-4537.00211.

Morgan Park High School. Morgan Park High School Chicago Public Schools. www.morganparkcps.org. (accessed: February 4, 2016).

Moynihan, D. P. 1965. *The Negro family: The case for national action.* Washington, DC: US Department of Labor.

National Center for Education Statistics. 1995, June. *Extracurricular participation and student engagement.* Washington, DC: NCES.

National Center for Education Statistics. 2016, May. *Racial/ethnic enrollment in public schools.* Washington, DC: NCES.

National Commission on Excellence in Education. 1983. *A nation at risk: The imperative for educational reform.* Washington, DC: US Government Printing Office.

National Reading Panel. 2000. *Teaching children to read: An evidence-based assessment of the scientific research literature on reading and its implications for reading instruction.* Washington, DC: National Institute of Child Health and Human Development. www.nichd.nih.gov/publications/pubs/nrp/documents/report.pdf.

Ostashevsky, L. 2016. Despite advances, racial achievement gap widens. *Courier Journal.* May 21, 2016.

President Obama's Farewell Address. www.nytimes.com/2017/01/10/us/politics/obama-farewell-address-speech.html, accessed January 12, 2017.

Tavernise, S. February 9, 2012. Education gap grows between rich and poor, studies show. *New York Times.* February 9, 2012.

Tucker, J. August 24, 2016. Good news on school test scores can't disguise achievement gap. *San Francisco Chronicle.* August 24, 2016.

Valenzuela, Angela. 1999. *Subtractive schooling: U.S.-Mexican youth and the politics of caring.* Albany: State University of New York Press.

About the Author

In her work with students, families, educators, and school leaders, Dr. Teresa Hill strives to make the school system work for every child. She is devoted to eliminating the achievement gap and ending what she has termed "failure as a default." Her motto is "All children can learn . . . period."

Dr. Hill has earned bachelor's, master's, and doctoral degrees in elementary education and educational administration and foundations from Illinois State University, where she researched the achievement gap. She began her education career teaching a kindergarten class of thirty-one students in Peoria, Illinois. Since then, she has served as an assistant principal, principal, assistant superintendent, and superintendent in a variety of school districts.

Dr. Hill consults with educational leaders, provides professional development, assists educators and school leaders with structured school improvement planning, and presents at state and national education conferences. She lives in Illinois with her husband, Archbishop A. Q. Hill, pastor of the St. Michael House of Prayer Church of Chicago, and their son, David.